The Tandem Book

The Tandem Book

Angel Rodriguez
and
Carla Black

INFO NET PUBLISHING
SAN CLEMENTE, CALIFORNIA

Cover design by Karen Fong
Cover photo by Mark Hanauer
Frontispiece photo by Steve Essig;
models: Kristen Carnes, Paul Rahmes

Typographical design
using Lucida, Lucida Sans, and Forte
by Robert Biddle of Artefac

Info Net Publishing
P. O. Box 3789
San Clemente, CA 92674

Telephone: (714) 489-9292
Fax: (714) 489-9595
E-mail: infonetpub@aol.com

Library of Congress Catalog Card Number 94-79071
ISBN 0-924272-03-1

Contents

Acknowledgements

The authors and publishers would like to thank the following individuals and organizations for their significant contribution in compiling The Tandem Book.

GREG SIPLE **and the Adventure Cycling Association,** for providing advise, guidance and Greg's skills as a photographer and interviewer in compiling the tandem profiles that appear throughout this book, as well as photos appearing on other pages, listed below. STEVE ESSIG, who provided the frontispiece photo, and KRISTEN CARNES AND PAUL RAHMES, the tandem couple appearing in the photo. Paul also served as associate editor in *The Tandem Book*. **The Tandem Club of America** (TCA) for providing guidance and a list of tandem clubs worldwide. *Tandem Magazine* for providing technical assistance and photographs. ESTELLE GRAY and the other personnel of **R + E Cycles** in Seattle, Washington for expert advise. BILL MCCREADY of Santana Tandems for his contributions of time in reviewing The Tandem Book manuscript and his expert advise and direction.

The following individuals and organizations generously provided photos and illustrations for *The Tandem Book*:

Green Gear Cycling, Inc./Bike Friday for page 4; Greg Siple, Adventure Cycling Association, for pages 6, 12, 21, 28, 32, 35, 44, 48, 59, 60, 84, 124, 130, and 133; the authors for pages 17, 26, 36, 62, 67, 105, 111, and 126; Montague Corporation for pages 30 and 137; Cycletote Corporation for page 39; Ryan Recumbents, Inc., for page 71; Advanced Transportation Products, Inc., for page 93; and *Tandem Magazine* for pages 97, 98, 134, 138, and 141

Introduction

THERE'S SOMETHING SPECIAL about riding together—really together, on a tandem. Tandem riding is unique in bicycling because you share completely the events of the day. From the same perspective, at the same moment. You're together on the hard grind up the hill, and you share the elation of the descent. When you are riding well, when everything clicks and you're feeling good, the tandem flies down the road. And through everything, you can enjoy conversation in a way that just isn't possible on a pair of single bikes.

A tandem is any bicycle that two or more people pedal. Webster's definition is a little more confining: "One behind the other, in single file; a bicycle with two seats and sets of pedals placed tandem." For our use, a tandem can have more than two riders, and they don't have to be one in front of the other. Most tandems in the world fit Webster's definition, but there are quite a few triple tandems (and at least one quadruple and one quintuple, that we know of), and a number of manufacturers make side by side tandems.

So, who are tandem riders? If you went to an organized tandem ride you'd see people of all ages and all descriptions having fun. You can't generalize much further. Some riders are big, some are small, and many teams are both. Some are fast, and others aren't worried about it. Some are super-fit, while others ride occasionally. Maybe Mom and Dad have the baby in a trailer. Some persuasive parents get their teenagers out there ... or is it the other way around? Some folks have been riding their tandem for years. For others, the new bike arrived just in time for the event.

And the colors are dazzling. In addition to the brilliant bikes themselves, tandem teams like to get dressed up. Matching jerseys are almost required on special occasions (any outing of two bikes or more), and if the jerseys match the bike, so much the better. And some even have matching panniers to complete the ensemble.

Tandem teams come in all combinations but the most common team is a couple, with the man riding in front and the woman riding in back. In that arrangement, *he* is usually called the captain and *she* is usually called the stoker. Some like the terms driver and rider, pilot and navigator, or captain and rear admiral. You can choose your own titles; we'll stick to captain and stoker in the book. The captain steers, shifts, and brakes. The stoker pedals and enjoys the view. We refer to the captain as "he," and the stoker as "she" throughout the book, knowing that they don't apply to all tandem teams; it is only a convenient gender reference. Families, many racing duos, a sight-impaired husband, or a pair of friends all defy our norm. In fact, we break the norm quite often ourselves. Carla and I are about the same height, and there is nothing but habit to keep us from trading positions. In the last few years we have been breaking that old habit, and we take turns captaining. It gives each of us a better understanding of the other's position, and it gives Angel a chance to look around!

For all their variety, tandem riders have a common trait: They enjoy riding. Most are cyclists who have enjoyed bicycling for years before they invested in a tandem. They're good riders; they have fun, but they don't take chances with two riders on board. It's the tandem riders' special attention to good riding and their long-standing love of the sport that makes riding with other tandemists a real pleasure. And not least, two tandems make for even better conversation than one tandem!

Aside from everything else, people ride tandems for one basic reason: tandems are fun.

The intent of this book is to make tandeming more fun by reducing the guesswork of buying, riding, and maintaining a tandem—whether you ride a tandem now, or are just beginning to think about it. And when you enjoy tandeming enough to convince your friends to join you, this book will come in handy again. If there's anything more fun than tandem riding, it's tandem riding with friends.

Are you hesitant to try tandeming? You're not sure you'll get along? As the stoker, you don't know if you can pass up the view down the road? As the captain, it seems like too much work and added responsibility? Well, read on, and believe us when we say, "We wouldn't ride anything else!"

Being on the same bike, within a foot of your tandem-mate all day, isn't as confining as it might sound (at least you don't have to face each other!). Sometimes we ride for hours thinking our own thoughts, seeing the landscape our own way. Sometimes we concentrate on efficient riding, other times we're only thinking about what we're going to eat next. Often we talk about things that are reserved for quiet times; you can't really do that on single bikes.

As the stoker, Carla especially appreciates the freedom to look around. Some prospective stokers are concerned about not being able to see down the road. Carla says she sees more from the tandem than from her single bike, precisely because she doesn't have to look down the road to steer the bike. When the road curves, she gets a sweep of the landscape, and often notices things ahead on the road before Angel does. Once, we were riding a bit of dirt road in dry eastern Washington, and chose a concrete bridge for a lunch spot. As we rolled up to the rail, Carla asked in a voice full of fear and disbelief, "We're not stopping right here, are we?" Startled by her tone, Angel quickly asked, "Why not?" "Because it's too close to that rattlesnake!" She had glimpsed a snake sunning itself on the smooth concrete, which Angel had not seen as he concentrated on bringing the loaded bike to a halt. That was the fastest dismount we can remember! Anyway, stokers see a lot from their special perspective!

The people who appear in the portraits you'll see throughout the book were visitors to Adventure Cycling Association (formerly Bikecentennial) headquarters in Missoula, Montana. The Adventure Cycling Association encourages the use of the bicycle for adventure and discovery. They have developed maps of a network of touring routes all over the United States, and organize group cycling trips. Greg Siple, art director and an original founder, took their portraits, as he has of hundreds of visiting cyclists. The tandemists answered a list of questions about themselves and tandeming for us. We asked what they like most about tandeming, what is hardest to get used to, and what advice they had for new tandemists.

The most telling responses were to the question, "What do you like best about tandeming?" Every team said that they liked the togetherness, the conversation, and the teamwork. What about the speed, about showing off to singles on downhills, about setting personal records? Admittedly, going fast is fun, but simply enjoying bicycling with someone you enjoy is the real reason most people keep riding.

Each team had a different comment on what was the hardest thing to get used to. Many of the riders were long distance tourists, and the fully-loaded tandem felt unusual for a while. Stokers said that they had to learn to keep rather still, and make no sudden movements. Captains had to tell the stoker about everything that was coming up.

Their advice to new teams was, "Talk, talk, talk, talk." Communicate everything. They suggested that you trade positions, if possible, to see how the other person feels. And be patient—you'll get it!

When asked if tandeming is for everybody, they said, "No!" You can't ride with someone you don't like, or who you argue with. You need a little extra trust and patience. As one team said, "If you can wallpaper together, you can tandem together." True. But you probably don't have to be *that* patient!

Tandem riding is obviously not the same as riding alone. It takes time and miles in the saddle for tandeming to become second nature. You can expect the first ride to feel a bit strange, but remember your first bike ride without training wheels? It was probably fun and full of excitement, but it doesn't even compare to how much you enjoy cycling now. Tandeming is fun right from the start, and the fun grows with every ride!

Your First Ride

YOUR FIRST tandem ride may be your most memorable. To make the memory a good one, you have to overcome some very natural concerns about getting on the same bike together. The captain might be a bit tense due to the extra size and weight of the bike and the extra person on board. And the stoker might be leery about trusting herself to the untried captain. From our experience getting started and helping others get started, we can offer these suggestions and tips to make sure you have a great first ride.

Start with Experience

The ideal introduction to tandeming is for each member of the new team to go out separately, riding as stoker, with an experienced captain on a tandem that fits properly. Then, after each has had a little experience with a veteran tandem rider, the new team can go out together. This bit of advice may sound like common sense, but perhaps some of the reasons don't seem as apparent.

By being a stoker for a while, the captain-to-be will be able to appreciate the anxiety and frustration any stoker feels on the first ride. For a new stoker, getting on a tandem and having no control over where the machine goes is something that takes getting used to. Every new captain should know how it feels to relinquish physical control of the bicycle to someone else. Riding on the back shows the new captain that communicating his intentions to the stoker is essential.

For the new stoker, riding with an experienced captain helps build confidence in trusting someone else to control the bicycle. The experienced captain can ride a straight line and handle the bike with confidence, keeping the tandem from feeling wobbly, a common complaint of first-time tandem teams. The ride will be smoother and less disconcerting for the new stoker if the captain is experienced. Losing the view straight down the road and totally trusting the captain is something that the stoker has to get used to ... slowly. It will take a little time, so if you don't feel one hundred percent comfortable on your first ride as a stoker, don't give up!

Once each half of the tandem team has taken a successful ride with a veteran tandem rider, they have confidence that riding a tandem can be smooth and easy, even before they first ride together. Each realizes that the less-than-solid feeling they might at first have on the tandem is due to inexperience, and not the tandem itself. Once they've ridden with an experienced captain, new tandem riders know that tandem riding is indeed fun and easy. The new team is more likely to enjoy the process of improving their riding proficiency as they get used to the machine and to riding together.

Bill McCready has put a lot of thought into what the first ride should entail for each member of the new tandem team. As founder and president of Santana Cycles, one of the top tandem manufacturers in the United States, he conducts regular hands-on presentations for bike stores all over the country that sell his Santana tandems. He describes how he takes the prospective captain and the prospective stoker for very different kinds of first rides:

"For the stoker, we go for about a two-mile ride that's really pleasant," says McCready. "We don't go very fast; we don't go very far. I point out things to look at. I point out the buildings and architecture. The intent is to get her where she is really at ease on the bike."

"The captain's ride is a lot different," says McCready. "I show him what the stoker feels like if the captain acts like a jerk. I ride too close to parked cars, I speed too quickly through corners, and do a number of other things to cause him to realize that riding the tandem requires a little bit more than just riding his single bicycle."

In taking a new captain and new stoker out on their first separate introductory rides, McCready shows the possibly unconvinced stoker that tandem riding can be fun and pleasant. And he demonstrates to the captain the vulnerability a stoker feels in the hands of an insensitive captain. The new captain learns the responsibility of handling the tandem carefully and always being aware of the stoker. He learns that when he rides with the stoker's comfort in mind, tandem riding is more enjoyable for both of them.

Finding an available experienced captain and tandem the right size for a trial run might be a challenge. Find a retailer that maintains a stock of various-sized tandems available for test rides. The new captain should undertake a stint on the back of any tandem available, even if the fit isn't ideal. Breaking in the new captain on a ride with an experienced stoker helps, too. An experienced stoker knows how to pedal without a lot of extra motion, and can pass on some information about what she expects from the captain.

Who is the Captain and Who is the Stoker?

Most couples who ride tandems put the man in front, as captain, and the woman in back, as stoker. Three intrinsic qualities of tandems support that choice. One is that it takes more upper body strength to handle a tandem than it does to handle a single bike, and men usually have greater upper body strength than their partners. The second is that the tandem is easier to handle when the stoker is lighter than the captain,

*Enjoying a ride on a collapsible tandem,
Tule Lake, California, on the Northwest Tandem Rally.*

which again usually suggests that the woman be stoker. The side-to-side movements of a 125-pound stoker are easier to compensate for than the wiggles of a 250-pound stoker. That is true when the captain is big, but it is doubly true when the captain is small. Third is that the team is more aerodynamic when the taller rider is in front and the shorter stoker sits entirely within the captain's slipstream. Two other circumstantial reasons add to the predominance of men captains and women stokers. First, often the man has had more cycling experience than his partner, and is more comfortable captaining the big bicycle. And second, almost all tandems are bigger in the front than in the back, so almost all teams fit better in the standard male-captain, female-stoker arrangement.

But, as you can see from the discussion of who sits where, which is more of a guideline than a law of physics, there is no reason a smaller man or woman cannot captain the tandem with a heavier stoker. That is especially true when the bicycle fits, the captain is comfortable handling the tandem, and the stoker has a smooth pedaling style.

When you finally get to ride together for the first time, the pedals should be in-phase. "In-phase" (as opposed to out-of-phase) means that both sets of pedals are in the same position at the same time: when the captain's right foot is in the up position, the stoker's is too. With the pedals arranged in-phase, you will feel more co-ordinated on the tandem, at least at first. Later you might choose to ride out-of-phase. See Chapter 8 for a complete discussion of the merits of each arrangement.

Together, Finally

So finally you both get on the same tandem. Your first move is probably the trickiest: getting on and getting the bike rolling. Tandemists use one of two techniques to get going smoothly. Read over the following descriptions of the two methods, choose one, and talk through the motions before you approach the tandem. Both techniques work best if you are on flat ground, or better yet, on a slight downhill slope. Be sure that you have ample clearance of obstacles, like parked cars and other bicyclists. Both methods require that you take a few good strong pedal revolutions before you coast, in order to put your feet in the toe clips. Many first-ride tandemists are too tentative with first pedal strokes, or stop to get their feet in the toe clips before they have enough momentum. That leads to a moment of panic while they resume pedaling furiously or scramble to get a foot to the ground. Even now, if Carla lets up on the pressure a little too early, Angel blurts out, "Keep pedaling!" We don't remember ever aborting a launch, but those close calls keep us on our toes.

Communication is more important at the start-up than at any other time in a tandem ride (except perhaps the stop!). The

Photo by Greg Siple

The Tandem Book

key words are, "Ready?," "Ready!." The captain asks, "Ready?" and waits for, "Ready!" from the stoker before shoving off.

The first technique to get rolling smoothly, probably the most popular, is for the captain to straddle the tandem, supporting it with a wide stance, both feet on the ground, and holding both brakes. The stoker then steps over the tandem, sits on the seat, and positions her feet on the pedals. Both riders have to keep in mind that the captain is keeping the tandem balanced and holding the stoker up before they get going. Keep vertical! Then the captain places one foot on a pedal, lifts that foot to prepare for the first stroke, and shoves off the way he does on a single bike. Together, make the first few pedal revolutions strong and even to get the tandem moving. Then the captain can put his other foot in the toeclip. Each stage in the mount requires communication; the captain announces, "Ready?" when he has firm control of the bike, to let the stoker know she can get on and position herself. Then the stoker says, "Ready!" when she is settled and prepared for the start. If the captain needs to stop pedaling to get his foot in the toeclip, he says, "Coast!"

The second method, the one we use, is to have both riders mount at the same time, as if they were each on a single bike. The captain gets on first, and holds both brake levers. Both riders put one foot on the left (or right) pedal, lift the pedal as high as it comfortably goes, push off together, and use the power from that first stroke to get rolling. They continue to pedal with a few strong, smooth revolutions before coasting, or even easing up on the pressure to get the other foot in the toeclip.

The advantage of the first method, where the stoker gets on the tandem first, is that the stoker provides constant power while the captain mounts up, rather than both fumbling for the start at the same time. The advantage of the second, where both get on at the same time, is that the captain does not have to hold the stoker, delicately balanced, on the stationary tandem. We like the joint mount because we are able to do it comfortably. It is simpler, and it puts less stress on the captain. Carla likes it because she feels more like a partner instead of a passenger—a small point, but our motto is, "Keep the stoker happy!"

The dismount is nearly as important as the mount. Do all of the steps in the reverse order. If you use the first method, where the captain holds the bike for the stoker to get on, she should remain comfortably seated until the tandem comes to a full stop. If you use the second method, and shove off together, you have to decide which foot you will put down in the dismount. Decide well in advance of the actual stop, to avoid an embarrassing and possibly painful end to your trip. In both methods, the captain must make sure the stoker is off and away before he swings his leg over the bike to dismount. The stoker is likely to get a swift kick if the captain dismounts before she is well clear!

For your first ride, choose a route with little traffic. Avoid hills so you can get the feel of the bike without having to shift a lot. Start out in a low gear and resist the urge to go fast and work hard. Take it easy, in terms of both traffic and hills, until you're both comfortable on the tandem.

Talk a lot and communicate your feelings and reactions as you go along. Tell the other person how it feels when you go around corners, how it feels when you stop and get going again, whether you like the cadence (how fast you are pedaling), whether the tandem seems steady or not. Talk about everything. When your reactions and impressions are out in the open, you can adjust your riding to make the other person more comfortable. Maybe the stoker is trying to steer the tandem, by leaning her weight as she does her single bike, and it is affecting the captain's ability to control the tandem. Say something! Maybe the captain is taking corners too fast for the stoker's comfort. Tell him! Express to each other your general impressions of tandeming as you ride along. Every bit of information you give your partner will help to make the experience better.

Say it Loud

A tandem team is just that: a team. The captain isn't the driver with the stoker as passenger. They are partners. The captain should announce out loud, and in advance, all plans to shift and brake, especially when he intends to come to a complete stop. The stoker should request any shifting or braking she feels is necessary. The captain should be sure there are no surprises for the stoker. If the captain can't avoid a bump, he should announce it. From the stoker's point of view, the only thing worse than a bump is a surprise bump!

The vocabulary for announcing shifting, braking and bumps uses the very words you might naturally use. If an unavoidable bump is severe, the captain can say, "Up!" or "Lift!" and stop pedaling for a moment, allowing the stoker to lift herself off the saddle to avoid the worst of the jolt. Most teams develop their own system of communication, based on the stoker's need to know what is in store. If the stoker says, "You should have told me about that," both riders can agree on the signal for next time. If she says, "I could tell already, without you saying it out loud," then perhaps you can drop that particular warning. Be selective about dropping verbal clues, though; better safe than sorry when it comes to communication and coordination.

Some teams elaborate on the basic information to describe an "Up shift," or "Coasting," then "Braking." There are a few signals we use only periodically, when good timing counts. When we are shifting to the smallest chainring (a shift that works only when there is no pressure on the pedals), Angel calls, "No power." Carla pushes again immediately after the chain engages on the small chainring, without further comment. We use "Coasting" only when we are pedaling very fast, and the resulting stop might jolt the stoker. Carla usually announces that she is going to take a drink, since reaching for the bottle and twisting slightly to drink from it affects the steering. Sometimes Angel asks her to hold off until they've cleared an obstacle of some sort. For the same reason, Carla lets Angel know if she is going to sit upright, or if she just wants to wiggle (the old bottom needs a little relief sometimes!).

For us, tandem riding keeps getting better and more fun as we become a better team on the bike. After long experience in telling each other about every motion and intent, some of the verbal communication has dropped off. We rely on other hints: when the cadence slows, a drop of the captain's shoulder as he reaches for the lever indicates an upcoming shift. We rarely mention braking except in unexpected situations.

Out in the Streets

When you're in traffic, ride conservatively, and don't sprint for traffic lights. Don't avoid putting a foot down at stop signs. While riding a single bike, you can make many traffic decisions in a fraction of a second; you can stop at a stop sign without putting your foot down, check for traffic, and if necessary, slip your foot to the ground instantly. It's not so easy on a tandem! You pretty much have to plan to put a foot down at each stop sign, look for traffic, and remount.

Make route decisions together well in advance; snap decisions are not easy on a tandem. Riding a tandem is a little like driving an oversize vehicle: If you're set up for a right turn, you have to go through with it. You can't change your mind as easily as if you were riding a nimble single bike. It isn't hard to plan ahead, especially if you are riding on familiar routes. Just agree on taking the normal route to Green Lake or wherever, and discuss variations a few blocks ahead of time.

Every decision on a tandem, ranging from the cadence you keep to which direction you're going to turn, has to be a joint decision. Some decisions, such as the ultimate destination and where you're going to stop for a break, are joint decisions whether you're on a tandem or riding singles. But the more touchy subjects in tandem riding are related to cadence, position on the road, and traffic behavior. Those are things each of you could handle differently if you were riding singles. Discuss traffic situations ahead of time, as you approach a particular intersection, for example. Or decide in advance to stop at stop signs every time. By reducing snap decisions, you can glide through any neighborhood like pros.

We have been riding tandems long enough that when we ride our singles we ride in the same gear as each other! That didn't come naturally. It took lots of talking and compromising to develop a cadence that works for both of us. You will probably have to compromise with each other for a while until you find a cadence that suits both of you. If consistency is important, install a cyclo-computer with a cadence counter, and agree on a range that is acceptable.

With some precautions and patience, your first ride will definitely be fun. But even if every moment wasn't perfection itself, remember that tandem riding only gets better from here!

Grace and Gene Vilain, Bay Area, California

Seattle to New York

"The journey awakened us spiritually – that's one thing about touring on a tandem, we were able to do a lot of thinking and talking about our life." On a lighter note, "We've had our frontal lobotomies to qualify for this ride. We gave it all away – big bucks, nice apartment, and more, just to see the leaves change in the East. Just two more crazies from California."

Riding a Tandem

Power Output

POWERING A TANDEM is a fifty-fifty proposition, but only in terms of effort, not in terms of raw power. Generally, the riders put out an equal percentage of their individual capability. While cruising, by spoken or tacit agreement, each person's power output might be fifty percent of what they're capable of. While climbing a steep hill, each rider might be at eighty-five percent of his or her maximum. However, the stronger person may be doing sixty percent of the total work, and the other person forty percent. That is what teamwork is about.

When we are riding, sometimes one of us wants to work very hard. But perhaps the other doesn't feel as enthusiastic. Thanks to the tandem, we just follow our individual inspirations, the speedster putting it all into pedaling, and the other rider maintaining the power level. We can each expend whatever effort we want while still riding together. This is what makes tandeming such a satisfying thing: you can be together even when you're in different moods.

City Riding

Riding a tandem in urban areas requires more communication than cruising across the countryside. Some riders have the patience to tackle city streets by tandem, and others don't.

You have to try it a few times to know which category you fall into. If you can stay calm and civil while riding in the city, congratulations! If it all seems more trouble than it is worth, don't let it bother you—just don't ride the tandem in the city any more than you have to. The following suggestions will help you deal with tandeming through the busy streets, whether or not you intend to make a habit of it.

As you approach each intersection you have to agree on whether you're going to make a complete stop, whether one or both of you will put a foot down, and when you'll make the dash across the intersection. When you ride a single bike in the city, you constantly make split-second judgments and decisions at stop signs, lights, and driveways. But when you're riding a tandem, you can't act as quickly and automatically. Both of you have to agree that you're going to stop, or that you're going to cross immediately, before that car gets any closer. You might want to have a standard practice for signs, lights, and other common situations. It is easier to set a policy that you will always stop at stop signs, for instance, instead of trying to judge the traffic situation as you approach, then stopping in a panic.

When you ride in the city, choose routes which are protected by stop signs controlling the side street traffic, so you don't have to make a judgment at every intersection. If your goal is to get out of town for traffic-free riding, choose a major route with a comfortable shoulder. Such a route is generally safer than neighborhood streets, and you'll make good time getting out of the congestion.

Drafting and Drafters

Drafting is the practice whereby one or more riders takes advantage of the wind break provided by a lead rider; a drafting group is called a pace line. As tandemists, you will undoubtedly have to face the issue of drafting. Everyone wants to draft a tandem! Tandems are very attractive lead vehicles, for two reasons: they go faster than single bikes, and the draft, or pocket of still air behind a tandem, is bigger than that of a single. How you deal with drafters, or whether you accept them at all, is up to you.

By riding with your friends you can work out what your individual road rules will be. At first, you shouldn't let other cyclists draft or ride too closely; make sure you have all the elbow room you need to handle the tandem. You need a little more space while you're getting used to the tandem, and the added tension of thinking about someone drafting closely behind you can take a lot of the fun out of a pleasure ride.

If you choose to draft, do it after you are very familiar with the braking and handling characteristics of the tandem. It takes longer to stop, and rock-dodging techniques do not transfer directly from your single to the tandem. If you draft a single, that cyclist has to adjust his riding style to guide a tandem around obstacles. As always, and more important on the tandem, you don't want to draft anyone you don't know and trust as a cyclist. The following position is more dangerous than the lead position, because if the wheels overlap and touch, the front wheel of the following bike can be deflected, possibly causing a fall.

A tandem moving along at a good clip looks attractive to cyclists who are trying to make time. Take on a drafter only when you want to. It is not worth the extra stress to have someone back there you don't want. If worse comes to worse, stop to take a rest and let the hanger-on continue.

All that cautioning taken into account, there is nothing quite as exhilarating as a tandem pace line. A group of three or four skilled tandem teams can make short work of a prairie head wind or a long gentle downhill. The stoker should find a constant effort level that most of the time maintains the distance from the next tandem, and the captain can fill in the gaps with a little extra effort, or back off by letting up a bit. The stoker cannot see the wheel in front clearly enough to participate in fine tuning the distance between you and the tandem ahead of you, so that's the role of the captain. Keep the communication going to find the effort level for the stoker. Then the stoker has to concentrate on producing an even power output.

Riding With Singles

Aside from drafting, when you're riding in a mixed group of single bikes and tandems, things go more smoothly when the single riders know what to expect from a tandem in their midst. Let the other riders know that emergency maneuvers and other quick motions take longer to execute for you on the tandem. In other words, no squirrelly riding should be allowed near a tandem. Also, the tandem will pick up speed going downhill much faster than a single, and go faster. The singles should leave you some space to pass them. You should leave the single riders space to pass you going up the other side, if the hill is long enough for you to lose momentum (which you have a lot of!). Often in rolling hills, the tandems and singles pass each other constantly. If you're on drafting terms, the single will have to wait for you at the top of the hill, and catch you there, instead of starting down and trying to catch you on the fly. You'll have to accelerate more slowly than usual to keep the drafter on. It's fun, but really it's more of a game than an efficient way for either of you to ride.

Speaking of rolling hills: that is where, we think, tandems really shine. Each downhill gives you lots of momentum to get up the next roller without nearly as much effort as a single. If you work at the top of the downhill to pick up as much speed as possible, you can often get up the other side without working at all. The effort might all come out in the wash, but we prefer working to go fast downhill instead of working hard to go slowly uphill!

These options in riding styles and techniques are unique to tandems because tandems are unique. With the effort and

Enjoying a ride in rain gear.

weight of two riders, tandems behave differently than singles. It's another one of those special things about tandems.

Uphills and Tandems

We get lots of questions and comments about hills from non-tandem cyclists. The lycra-clad, twenty-year-old bike racer says something like, "Sure, tandems are fast, but they really go slow uphill." Of course, that fellow dusts everybody uphill. What he and others don't realize is that if you are fast uphill riders on your singles, (you take pride in it), and if you practice on the tandem, you can climb with the best of them. As one pair of hill-jamming tandemists said, "Tandems don't climb hills—people do."

For us, and many tandemists, it's a matter of what we think is the best use of our energy. Why use up a big chunk of energy racing up a quarter-mile hill, when you could save it for covering a couple of miles somewhere else? Yes, we feel that we could individually get up the hills a bit faster. But we know for sure, that on any given day of riding, we could never finish as fast or as comfortably on our singles as on our tandem. We ride mostly in the West, and are used to climbing twenty-five miles at six percent grade; we just pick a comfortable gear and keep at it. The hills may be a bit slower, but they aren't any harder.

Fifteen years ago we climbed hills faster; but we did everything faster in those days. Going up hills is a matter of attitude. We enjoy hills. We know that many singles are going to pass us on a long uphill, but then we pass many singles, too. And we know that we'll catch them on the downhill. We have tandeming friends to whom it's important to go fast uphills. They do a great job of staying up with the best of the singles on the uphills, and giving them hell on the downhills. It can be done, and you can do it, if it is important to you. But if it's not, don't worry about it. Put it in a low gear, and enjoy the scenery.

Mountain Tandeming

Mountain tandeming is a lot of fun, especially if you like mountain biking. It is fun for all the same reasons road tandeming is fun: the joy of working together, of being together, of getting to the top at the same time. And of course, it can be fast if you're daring.

We enjoy mountain tandeming on dirt roads more than on trails. The tandem is surprisingly maneuverable on trails, and it can do some tricks that you can't on a single mountain bike, but we think the stoker gets the raw end of the deal on the trail. Like raw bottom end. It is hard for the stoker to anticipate the bumps and sharp curves of the trail, and just as hard for the captain to announce everything. Consequently, the stoker just hangs on, pedals, and doesn't dare sit down. We think that the fun of single-track mountain biking is in steering and maneuvering the bike through the obstacle course of a trail. From the back of the tandem, you can't enjoy the playful challenge of the trail.

In contrast, we enjoy dirt road riding on the tandem. A dirt road is usually smoother than a trail, and the captain can steer around the worst of the bumps. The fat tires, properly inflated (that means not too hard) provide a lot of cushioning, like on a single mountain bike. As stoker, when you're not worried about the next bump, or staying upright over the upcoming obstacle, you can enjoy the scenery and the fresh air of being out and away from the crowds. A mountain tandem is perfect for the dirt-road passes of Colorado and the West, for bird-watching expeditions, and for jaunts around town.

We have certainly done some trail riding, and enjoyed it's special challenges. As we mentioned earlier, tandems do a couple of things very well out on the trails. One of them is brake. A hazard of single mountain bike braking is going over the handlebars while clamping down on the front brake too hard. That just won't happen on a tandem! Even though you may be diving head-first off a steep precipice and gripping the brake levers for all you're worth, the back end of the bike just won't come off the ground.

Another trick that the mountain tandem does for you is roll over and through obstacles that will stop a lighter weight single bike in its tracks. The additional weight of the tandem carries you through sandy stream beds, over round river rocks, and through snow patches, as long as you have a little momentum going for you. Be careful not to bash into something that really is too big, because the extra weight that usually works for you can turn into a wheel-bending load if the tandem can't get up and over the obstacle after all.

Mountain tandems have a few limitations that singles don't, however. Leave the bunny-hopping to the experts. Unless you are a very good off-road rider, you will probably not be able to even lift the front wheel up over a curb. So you have to roll over or around everything in your path; your wheels are staying on the ground. Another difference is that the tandem's turning radius is somewhat longer than that of a single. It doesn't bother us particularly, because the only turns we can't make on the tandem are the steep switch-backs, and we don't always make those on singles.

The added weight gives you better traction in all situations. A tandem is less likely to skid on the steep downhills, as well as on the steep uphills. Fast, downhill cornering on dirt roads is something we don't do, so we can't say how it feels compared to a single. There are some risks which seem acceptable on a single, as long as you're the only one to suffer the consequences. As in road tandeming, the captain of a mountain tandem has the well-being of another person to consider all the time. For us, and for most tandemists, that added responsibility slows us down just a little bit, and lowers our risk-taking a notch.

Back in town, mountain tandems have a nice, solid feeling, and are easy to captain. Their stability puts new stokers at ease, and makes them more comfortable to ride in traffic, or where quick maneuvering might be necessary. One word of caution, however: If you ride a tandem with knobby off-road tires on pavement, you compromise handling much more than you do on a single mountain bike. The extra weight of the tandem puts stress on the side knobs of the tire while cornering; those knobs support the weight up to a certain point, and then they flex out from under the bike. That not only gives you a squishy ride, but it is dangerous if you pass the limit of what the tire can support. If you do ride a lot on pavement, choose tires with no knobs, or with short ones, especially on the outside edges.

Some tandems are sold as convertibles, from mountain to road configurations, and back again. The major differences between road tandems and mountain tandems are the weight and strength of the wheels, the handlebar design, and perhaps the gearing. Twenty-six-inch road wheels and tires are very common (we recommend them highly), and owning two sets of

Photo by Greg Siple

Bozeman, Montana, cyclists Ted Turner and David Schipper rode their Fisher Tandem to a 23-minute, 22-second finish in the men's tandem category at the Missoula Bicycle Club's Western Montana Hill Climb Championships.

wheels is an inexpensive way to enjoy both road and mountain tandeming. Compromise gearing is probably the way to go if you switch uses often, though owning a variety of chainrings will allow you to customize gearing for a long stretch of mountain riding or for a road riding vacation. Straight mountain handlebars, with additional bar-ends to allow you to change your hand position, may be satisfactory for road riding. Or, depending on the kind of off-road riding you do, drop-style touring bars might work just fine. You can change bars, of course, though that is a more involved process than changing wheels.

Riding a Tandem **21**

The most complementary uses for a mountain tandem are off-pavement riding and touring. The strong twenty-six-inch wheels are perfect for touring, and the design and fit of a mountain tandem make it a very stable and easy-to-handle touring bike. We would change seats, as well as wheels or tires, since we use very different saddles on the road and mountain bikes.

Riding with or as a Blind Stoker

Tandems provide the perfect (and usually the only) opportunity for sight-impaired people to ride bicycles. Just as with sighted people, bicycling offers blind people a new view of their surroundings. Everything seems just a little different by bicycle. Hills gain new importance, both on the way up and on the way down. An aromatic vine or a rustling tree seem fresh and new. The smells of dampness and dryness, the warmth of the sun along a lake in the spring, or the cool shade of a boulevard in the heat of summer—all take on a different feel. And you know that nothing in the bakery tastes quite as good as it does when you've earned it with a few miles behind you.

These impressions and small joys are special enough to keep sighted riders coming back for more. To a blind person, the new view could be more than just a little shift in perspective. A blind person has to walk with care; simply getting around takes the better part of his or her attention.

Tandeming relieves the stoker of the basic chore of navigation, and that is no small thing to a blind person. The stoker is free to smell, feel, and hear the surroundings. Many blind people have never moved so fast outdoors or outside of a car. The speed can be scary (a feeling not limited to blind stokers!), but it can be exhilarating, once the stoker learns the feel of the tandem and develops trust in the captain.

Of course, tandeming opens up the world of competitive cycling to the blind stoker, too. While sight-impaired tandem racing is just getting off the ground here in the U.S., tandem racing has been established in Europe for a decade. Many of the races are open only to teams with a sight-impaired stoker (usually on a country-by-country basis), but many others are open to all comers. In both cases, the competition is extremely demanding, but the open races allow the blind athlete to race against the best, leaving his or her handicap behind. Few sports offer such a splendid opportunity for a blind athlete to reach the pinnacle of his sport, and of his ability. See the Tandem Racing section for more information about racing for sight impaired stokers.

Touring and day riding by tandem gives blind stokers the opportunity to enjoy cycling in much the same way most of us do: To be outdoors, to enjoy the exercise, to appreciate the teamwork of tandeming, to scarf down a big plate of spaghetti while telling lies and truths about how fast, how far, how much fun.

If you have the opportunity to captain for a blind stoker, you should keep a few things in mind. The experience level of your stoker is the most basic consideration. This is true no matter who your stoker is, but if you have a blind stoker who is new to tandeming, he or she is probably new to bicycling altogether. This will probably be your first stoker who is not familiar with the feel of bicycling at all. When you first go out, take it easy. Keep talking about what to expect, try to explain what the ride will feel like, announce turns and suggest that he or she should try to keep still, not try to lean or fight the lean through the corner. Try not to use busy streets where cars will have to pass closely; that is scary enough from the back of the tandem, and if your stoker is not used to being in the street at all, it could be worse than scary.

It is possible that your new stoker has not done anything athletic before (like so many sighted people), so don't just show up for the regular Saturday morning ride and expect to whip off a quick thirty miles. Anything over five miles is a lot for many people who have bikes and ride them periodically, and even more so for those who haven't sat on a bicycle seat, nor had their legs go around unmercifully mile after mile. Just take it easy; offer the stoker the kind of excitement which will get him to come back for more, not the excitement which will keep him home.

Many sight-impaired stokers are the husbands in a husband/wife team. The wife, who is probably smaller, is the captain. They ride a tandem which is the same size front and back, or a custom bike which is smaller in the front. Actually, more small-captain tandems are made for sighted couples, when the man is smaller and is the captain. So the tandem itself is not a problem. Any tandem can be made to fit a little better with easily-changed parts such as handlebar stems and seatposts. See the section on Parts for more information.

Touring with a Tandem

Touring by tandem can be one of the most enjoyable types of bicycle riding. There's nothing quite like heading out under the combined power of two people and not coming back. You can take a loaded tandem on steep descents at over fifty-five miles per hour with confidence! You can cruise a bit faster than you would on your singles, you can talk anytime you want, and best of all, you arrive at the same time. And from the stoker's point of view, there's no better way to see the countryside than to let the other guy do the driving.

Take a Shake-Down Trip

Before taking a long trip on a tandem, be sure that you are comfortable riding together. Touring itself offers enough novelty that you shouldn't be learning how to ride a tandem, too!

Take an overnight trip or two. When we're loaded for a weekend of camping we are carrying nearly as much stuff as we did when we rode our tandem across the country in 1980. There isn't a whole lot you can leave behind just because you're only going be out a few days. You still need the tent and sleeping bags, the cook pots, extra clothes, and something to read. So you can learn a lot about tandem touring even on overnight outings.

Pack lightly. Use both front and rear panniers.

The tandem will handle differently once you put an extra sixty to one hundred pounds on the racks. And the handling changes, depending on where you put the weight. We found that moving just a few pounds from the front bags to the rear bags, or vice versa, can make a big difference in the stability of the tandem. On an overnight trip you can experiment with weight distribution on the tandem. You can try loading the weight differently and compare the handling characteristics. Even when the bike is loaded perfectly, it will certainly handle differently than without the load!

We learned our lesson the hard way. When we headed out on our two-month trip across the country, we had never loaded the bike for an overnight trip, and we didn't know anyone else who had, either. When we first got on the fully-loaded tandem, we weren't sure this great idea of ours was going to work; the tandem seemed to have a mind of its own. But we couldn't turn back and tell everyone we weren't going, that we couldn't load a tandem! It took us a while to get used to the difference, and the first few days were really discouraging. We shifted some weight, sent some extra stuff home, and kept going. Needless to say we got the hang of it, and it turned out to be the best bike ride we've ever taken.

Don't Overdo It

Plan your miles per day conservatively at first. Give yourselves time to get acquainted with the new handling characteristics of the loaded tandem, without being anxious about how many miles you have yet to go. Remember, as well as you two get along, you're going to be very close together on any tandem trip. It is easy to get grumpy over the little stuff if you're tired or hungry, so plan shorter days at first, and don't push too hard.

Don't worry too much about being in great shape for a tour. Being comfortable on a tandem together, and making sure the tandem is comfortable for each of you, is more important than being super fit for a tour (of course, being in shape isn't a bad idea, either). Plan your daily distances to be a bit shorter than what you're used to on one-day rides. If your tour is longer than five days, you'll have time to get stronger as you go. Technically, tandem touring is a lot like bicycle touring on a single bike. There is one obvious difference: the amount of gear you can carry. You may be thinking even now, "How on earth can we fit two people's clothes and camping gear onto one bike?" Unfortunately, there are no magic tricks.

Packing

Pack lightly. Use both front and rear panniers, and put your tent and sleeping bags on the rear rack. Hang a handlebar bag on the front. Use two sets of big panniers if you have to, but it might not be necessary. Even the biggest panniers will get filled

with "essential" stuff. Consider something smaller than the biggest panniers you can find. You will probably appreciate the lighter load, and won't miss those "essentials."

Our cooking gear fits into one small pannier; our toiletries and medicines in another; and each of us has a large pannier for whatever we want: clothes, paperback book, letter writing equipment, and other personal items. Your tandem companion doesn't have to know and shouldn't care what's in your bag, as long as it doesn't include a big block of lead. Once, as we were buying groceries, we arrived at the check-out counter with two jars of mustard. As we discussed who had to give up their favorite kind, the checker, who could see that we were cycling, said, "Why don't you each just carry your own?" We looked at each other and realized that was just what we should do. It was certainly what we would do if we were on single bikes, so why not on the tandem? Each tandem rider needs a little privacy and autonomy, even if you are both in this together.

For light touring, when you're staying in hotels and eating hot meals in restaurants, you'll probably have all the space you need in four medium-sized panniers, or in two big ones. If you're riding from lodging to lodging, without sleeping gear or a full complement of cooking gear, your packing limits will not be so tight. You'll still have to be careful, and if necessary, plan to do laundry a bit more often.

What to Take

On trips of a week or more, we carry about sixty pounds of clothes, cooking utensils, and camping gear in one set of big panniers and one set of small ones. We pack lightly (some tourists on singles carry as much weight as we have on the tandem), allowing two pairs of riding shorts apiece (wash one, wear the other), and a pair of off-the-bike shorts. We take three shirts for riding, and one off-the-bike shirt. A couple of pairs of underwear, socks, cleated shoes, lightweight sneakers, and a warm shirt for on or off the bike completes the list. For warmth on and off the bike, we use polypropylene tights and nylon wind breakers. We carry rain gear only in colder months or on tours in higher elevations. You will find room for it, but if you don't like the sauna effect of wearing rain gear in warm weather, don't bother to bring it!

Enjoying a tandem tour.

The list of clothing we mentioned above keeps us comfortable on camping trips. Depending on your preferences and the opportunities for living it up a little, you might include some respectable off-the-bike clothes for a night of luxury at a hotel, or dinner in a nice restaurant.

In one front pannier we carry a hiking stove (which burns almost anything—unleaded gasoline is convenient while on the road), a small stew pot, a skillet, some spices, cooking and eating utensils, unbreakable glass (Corelle) bowls, cups, and a small coffee-making kit. The other front bag holds the tool kit, soap, shampoo, light-weight towels, sunscreen, first aid kit, toothbrushes, and space left over for whatever food we are carrying. Of course, apples get tucked in anywhere, and bread is gently secured on the outside.

Strap on your tent, sleeping bags and ground pads with non-elastic straps for a really secure load. Stretch a couple of bungee cords over the straps to hold jackets or other extra clothing, to keep them handy throughout the day. We make it a point of pride to not look like a Gypsy caravan, and stow most everything inside the bags. Our walking shoes are handy under the bungee cords with the wind breakers, and lunch supplies ride the few blocks to the park carefully stacked on.

Tools and the Ten Cycling Essentials

For day rides, all you need are the tools and spare parts to help you and your tandem get back home if you have mechanical trouble on the road. They might be a cellular phone and enough cab fare! But for most people that isn't the most convenient option. Estelle Gray, owner of R+E Cycles in Seattle, Washington, one of the biggest tandem shops in the country, says that what you really need are the ten cycling essentials on every ride, tandem or otherwise. These items aren't in order of importance, because they are all essential.

1. Helmet
2. Water
3. Some food or energy bars
4. Wind breaker
5. Money, including change for a phone call
6. Pump
7. Patch kit, tire levers and extra tube
8. Basic set of Allen wrenches, including a wrench to remove your rear wheel
9. Eye protection
10. Identification, with medical information

The eleventh essential is:

11. If you ride at night, use lights.

If you are going out on a ride of a few days or more, we think you need the following tools in addition to the Ten Essentials.

Spare spokes and a spoke wrench *(practice at home first)*
Freewheel tool
Chain tool
Five-inch Vise Grips *(original brand only; accept no substitutes)*
Spare gear and brake cables *(be sure to carry the longest one)*
Tools to adjust the front chain tension

For very long or extended trips, arrange to have spare chains and freewheels sent to you every three thousand to four thousand miles. Include in these care packages any other stuff you might need that is particular to your tandem.

Marilyn and George Mathison, and Muffin, Park Ridge, Illinois (now Hendersonville, NC)

Anacortes, Washington to Bar Harbor, Maine

"This is a celebration of our 25th anniversary and my husband's retirement. In addition, we are bringing our dog Muffin along as our travel-ing companion." George says, "When you're tandeming, you can't crash into each other, you can't get lost from each other, and you can talk to each other. That's the best part. Tandeming is the only way to go." About Muffin, "The bike won't run without a dog."

Riding Tandems with Children

IN OUR FIRST YEARS of tandem riding, we pedaled many miles with a family who rode a pair of tandems. The mom's stoker was the older girl, six years old, and dad had the four-year-old girl as his stoker. At that age, their little legs spun around rather idly while they chatted with us. Once in a while, mom or dad would ask for a little help on a hill, and the kids would put some effort into powering the tandem. In the meantime we played games, counted white horses, sang songs, and told stories. Riding tandems allowed the family to spend the day riding together, and allowed us to enjoy the company of all of them, including the girls. Thanks to the tandems, the parents didn't have to give up cycling just because the kids were young, and the girls learned to appreciate the special pleasures of cycling.

By riding tandems as a family, you don't have to wait until your children have the skills and endurance for a full day ride on single bikes, and they are developing those skills from your example. Longer and longer rides help build up the childrens' endurance, and you don't have to worry whether they can make the distance alone.

A tandem can be modified, with an attachment called a kid-back adapter, for a child's short legs and arms. It consists of a crankset which is clamped to the rear seat tube, and is connected to the original crankset with an extra chain. It usually includes a handlebar extender which puts the bars closer to the seat, allowing a child to reach them comfortably.

The kidback adapter consists of an extra set of cranks bolted onto the stoker seat tube. The kidback cranks are special: only five inches long. They are connected via a chain to an additional chainring bolted to the inside of the rear, left-hand crank. Add a long stoker stem, or turn drop bars toward the child, so the young stoker can reach the rear bars, and you're ready to roll!

Another way to help young stokers fit a tandem is to add blocks to the pedals. Leave the tandem in its original configuration; just make the pedals come up to the child's shorter legs.

Family Tandem Options

A family has a number of tandem riding options. One tandem is enough if you have one child, or if the other youngsters ride their own singles. Many families with two kids ride two tandems, each parent with a child on the back. This is ideal even if the children are old enough to ride singles, because the tandems allow you to take long or fast rides. Some families invest in one good tandem and one inexpensive tandem. When the family rides together, they take both bikes, and when the parents ride without the kids, they ride the good bike.

Other families have acquired three tandems, two inexpensive bikes for when they're out with the kids, and one adult-only bike. With three tandems, all the combinations are open. How you choose to accommodate the family on tandems depends on the size of your family, the children's ages, and your desire to ride tandems. If tandeming is your favorite kind of cycling, and you ride a lot, you'll undoubtedly end up with more than one tandem. Otherwise, one might be enough.

TOSRV Photo by Greg Siple

When you are choosing the tandem to use as a kidback bike, keep the following in mind: the kidback adapter is clamped onto the rear seat tube. If the clamp is not of the highest precision, and most aren't, uneven fit will destroy paint and deform a thin seat tube. The effects won't be immediately visible, but you shouldn't buy your dream bike and then subject it to a cheap kidback adapter. Because permanent frame damage from an ill-fitting kidback adapter is a possibility, we recommend that you contact the builder of your tandem before installing this popular accessory.

There are a few triple tandems out there. On a triple, a three-person family can ride together: three seats, three cranks, three handlebars, on a machine that is just a bit longer and heavier than a standard tandem. It takes a pretty committed family—or rather a committed youngster—to make good use of a triple. If you do choose a triple, consider how long it will fit your child, and if your child will want to ride with you every time you want to take the tandem out. More often in a

Triple kid back

three-person family, one parent rides along on a single while the other two ride the tandem.

Seventy-Pound Jet Engines

At first, the youngest kids don't contribute a lot to their own propulsion, but we've seen seven-year-olds who were such speed demons that they were out of the saddle and cranking at every rise in the road. Many captains say that children are powerhouse stokers; it is known that children have a better weight-to-strength ratio than adults. Lots of parents say their kids hate to be passed by anyone, and when somebody starts to move ahead, the seven-year-old jet engines kick in. We know parents who get pooped out by the pace their kids want to set!

If the kids are goofing off in the back, and you're not getting any help, the solutions are a varied as the kids themselves. Maybe daydreaming is okay sometimes, but at other times, when you really need some help from back there, you'll have to try incentives suited to the individual. You can offer a special treat at the next rest stop, in the form of special food or dime-store toys. One mother we met put together a bag of little gift-wrapped knick-knacks, and they stopped for a little celebration every ten miles.

The two of you can make up a code word for when you really want some help, and you're not kidding. Though they might like to go fast, kids have short attention spans, and don't pick up the subtle clues from a tired parent that they have to keep working. You'll have to work out your own incentive plan, based on the goals that are important to your child.

Of course, bicycling is supposed to be fun, so plan your mileage so you're not pushing your kids past their limits. Many parents are careful not to take the kids out in uncomfortable weather; they make sure that the kids look forward to a bike ride, instead of feeling like it is imposed on them.

Food and Clothing

We have friends who put kids on the back of the tandem when they are three and a half years old. The primary limit is how long the kids can stay awake. With a short attention span and conditioning to fall asleep in a trailer (where they ride for the first three and a half years), their first rides aren't too long. But before long, the whole family takes adult-length tours with only a few special considerations.

Food is one of those. By the time children are eight and ten years old, they can eat more on bike rides than their parents! Many kidback tandems have a special cup rigged up on the handlebars, and the kids have something to eat anytime they want. A variety of food is important, including favorite snacks, since if the stuff gets boring, they won't eat anything. And you know that a hungry kid is a grouch, at best!

Children may need encouragement to eat and drink enough. With the distraction of cycling they may not realize that they are hungry or thirsty until they have used up their (small) bodily stores of energy. Plan lots of stops for resting and eating—every twenty minutes for young children, and up to an hour for teenagers. It is much easier to prevent deep-down hunger and thirst than it is to revive a worn-out child.

Clothing is another special consideration. Because of their smaller size, children lose heat faster, and they don't warm up while riding in quite the same way adults do. Start out with lots of clothes on the children, and let them decide when to take off layers.

Children's cycle clothing is somewhat hard to find, though a few manufacturers make items for children. Many cycling moms have become cycling seamstresses, producing mini-jerseys, tights, and shorts. And as long as current fashion trends hold, there are lycra shorts in all sizes (though without padding) in the pop-fashion shops in the mall. Covering the saddle with a gel-type pad could be the right combination.

Children's rain gear is available at your local bike shop or outdoor clothing and camping retailers. If you don't intend to ride in the rain, and ready-made rain gear wouldn't get much use, keep emergency outer wear in the bottom of the bike bag; a garbage bag with a head-hole, arm-holes, and a string for a belt serves in a pinch. Though not a replacement for real rain wear, this makeshift covering will be better than nothing as you head for shelter.

Don't forget helmets. They are essential for both adults and children. Children's and infants' helmets are available in most shops, and mail-order. Hopefully kids already wear helmets whether they're on the tandem, in the trailer, or riding their own bikes on the sidewalk. Some state laws mandate helmets.

Keep Kids' Options Open

On your own tour you can choose your route and riding schedule to suit your children's abilities, an important element for a successful ride with children. However, lots of kids ride week-long organized rides either on tandems or on their own bikes. On organized rides you can't take a lay-over day, and you can't pick the route. On those rides, the happiest kids are the ones who have the choice not to ride every mile. They have a car along as back-up transportation. Maybe one of the parents drives, or sometimes the grandparents come along. The important thing is that the children have a choice. They can choose to ride only half the day, or they can opt to get in the car on a rainy afternoon. Sometimes they choose to continue in unpleasant conditions; but they call the shots. Kids who cycle when it is fun enjoy cycling.

Taking the kids along is rewarding for the whole family. As one young stoker after a week-long ride put it, "This is the best vacation I ever had."

We know a number of teen-age tandem teams. Mom and dad ride their tandem, and the kids ride their own, too. That lets the parents enjoy each other's company and pace, and lets

Cycle-Tote trailer

the youngsters enjoy the independence that a separate bike provides.

Tandems are the preferred bike for trailer towing because they are stable and allow both parents to share the chore. Lots of people hate towing a trailer behind their single—tandem couples will hardly notice the difference!

Trailers

The youngest children can come along in a trailer behind the tandem with enough space left over for the toys, food, and diapers. Overhead crib toys are popular with the really little ones. For the bigger kids, who need bigger toys, bring only those that can survive a tumble from the trailer. Parents report that kids are sometimes inspired to throw a toy out periodically. Keeping the cover on the trailer closed up will keep toys, fingers, and warmth inside—and weather and debris outside. However, all that said, if you ever looked inside a trailer with a kid in it, you probably saw him sleeping peacefully.

Helmets are a must on any bike ride, whether riding in a trailer or not. If your child is too young to support his head while wearing a helmet, strap a car seat into the trailer to keep his head from lolling too far to the side. The car seat also provides good over-the-shoulder seat belt protection.

Ride prepared for a child who might become motion sick. Until you try trailering, you just don't know. A little extra clean-up equipment could go a long way.

Always keep your bike well-maintained at home, and you won't have to make repair stops along the way. This is doubly important when you have a toddler or two along in the trailer. As one parent said, "Keeping an eye on children and fixing bikes don't mix." Especially alongside a road, so near traffic.

There are quite a few trailers on the market, and there's a good used market in some areas, too. Most parents prefer trailers which are designed for the child to be facing forward, with mom and dad in full view, and vice versa. Others prefer the rear-facing design, and feel that it better protects the child from rain and road debris. One youngster we met was kept pleasantly busy talking to following cyclists while she faced backwards, a fact that pleased her mother.

When selecting a trailer, be sure that the hitch allows the trailer to remain upright even if the bicycle tips over. The trailer design should also allow the trailer to remain upright if one of its wheels bumps up over a curb in a tight turn.

Consider using a bike flag because the trailer is lower to the ground than the bicycle that pulls it. The flag helps point out that your train is longer than it appears at first. A tandem with trailer is about eleven feet long.

Kids' Interviews

We have met a lot of young stokers on week-long organized tours, especially on Pedal Across Lower Michigan (PALM). PALM is more or less flat, and the daily distances are between thirty and fifty-five miles. The organizers cater to families, offering activities in the evenings, and pointing out swimming holes and playgrounds on the daily route sheet.

Jessica Dimino rode Ride Around Wyoming (RAW) with her dad, Jim, in 1990 when she was seven years old. She rode only as much as she wanted, then she got in the van with her mom, Judy, and Jim continued on his single bike.

Jessica says:

"The funniest thing about tandeming is going downhill. The hardest part is going uphill, but it is worth it to go down the other side. I work extra hard going up. I can reach the water bottle by myself, but we stop to eat. Big trips like RAW are really fun. This is the best vacation I ever had."

We met the Reed Family during the week-long Pedal Across Lower Michigan in 1990, when Sarah was eight and Nathan was four-and-a-half. Mother and father, Ellen and Mark, captain two kidback tandems. Nathan started riding when he was three-and-a-half. Since the first time he rode the tandem around the neighborhood, he wouldn't ride in the trailer anymore. Luckily, they had another tandem they could convert with a kidback.

Nathan says:

"The best thing about tandem riding is going fast. Macaroni is the best food."

Sarah says:

"I started riding when I was five. The best thing about tandeming is going fast with dad and passing people. The only good thing about riding in the rain is wearing a trash bag raincoat. I would rather not ride in the rain, but it isn't all that bad. We play letter games, like naming friends or animals (going through the alphabet on first letters). We also sing songs a lot. One special thing I get to do when we ride is eat Gorp. I like to go about thirty miles in a day."

We met the Havenga Family: Jim and Kay, Katie, 9, Jonathan, 7, and Laura, 4, on Pedal Across Lower Michigan in 1990. All the kids are stokers, though Katie rides her single a lot—the entire week of PALM. Jonathan rides stoker with dad, Laura usually rides in the trailer, though they take turns in the trailer and stoking.

Katie says:

"Tandem riding is more fun than single riding because your back doesn't get sore. You can change positions. My dad notices when I push extra hard. I think I could ride one hundred miles on a tandem. I can reach the food, and I pass it up to my dad."

We passed Jon and Jim with the trailer, and at that moment Jon was pedaling by himself.

Jonathan says:

"It was pretty hard to pedal by myself. Dad had to shift so I could do it. If I'm really pushing, dad knows it. I really like tandeming for a whole week. I like everything about tandeming. I keep food in my fanny pack, and I can eat anytime I want. I would tell other kids that tandeming is pretty easy—just do it."

The Wessel Walker family was also on PALM in 1990: Donna and Jim, Mary Elizabeth, 6, and Margaret, 3. Mary Elizabeth is the stoker for her mother or father.

She says:

"I am six years old. I started riding when I was five. I really like riding PALM. My favorite food is Pita bread, and we always stop to eat. But I can drink water while we're riding. The best part about tandem riding is that you get to work for real. The worst part is you can't sleep (like in the trailer). I like to ride about forty miles a day. To ride a tandem you have to know how to pedal and how to balance. I would tell other stokers to keep the captain happy by singing songs and talking, and not to forget to drink water."

Marshall & Pamina Haddock, Columbus, Ohio.

Astoria, Oregon to Yorktown, Virgina

Marshall and Pamina are a father-daughter team. Their tandem is a Counterpoint. She celebrated her 21st birthday on the road. Pamina wrote a lot about the trip, but the most amusing incident was while they were Moving east, "we were riding on a rather busy road through the Ozarks when a Hostess delivery truck went by. Two missiles flew out of it after it had passed us, and landed on the road ahead. We, of course, classed him as a bicycle-hating jerk until we realized he had tossed out Twinkies for our lunch."

Tandem Racing

TANDEM RACING is not what anyone could call a popular sport. Few people have seen a tandem race, and even fewer have actually raced tandems. Its obscurity is certainly not due to lack of speed, team work, or challenge. It's more exciting than single racing for riders and spectators alike. Cornering, maneuvering, and sprinting are all accentuated in tandem racing.

Nothing can match the pure raw power and speed of tandems in flat terrain, and when it comes to the gravity assisted mega-speed of the downhills, the singles can just forget it. What would be a dull flat section for singles is transformed to a thirty-five-mile per hour drag strip by racing tandems. What would be a gentle downhill slope for singles becomes a thrilling descent at over fifty miles per hour for racing tandems.

One of the most rewarding aspects of tandem riding, and particularly tandem racing, is good team work. The determining factor in a tandem race is not always youth and strength. Victory often goes to the team which works well together—to the team which has developed an unspoken communication, which doesn't waste time and effort in shifting and can read tiny, unspoken bits of communication passed forward and back. The ability to shift through twelve gears on an uphill and not miss a beat really shows teamwork, and makes a big difference at the finish line.

Most tandem racing teams comprise highly conditioned athletes, both in the men's categories and in mixed (male/female) team racing. They all share a sense of fun, too, since no one is going to make a career of tandem racing anytime soon. Some teams come from the tandem mountain bike world, where a few tandems compete with the single bike riders. Others are single bicycle racers who get together for the few tandem races. Tandem racing also allows a strong rider, who would otherwise not consider racing, to team up with a racing regular, and discover a new experience.

That doesn't mean that an inexperienced rider can just jump into a tandem race, even with an expert captain. The team has to ride together a lot and communicate well before they enter a race. They will enjoy themselves a lot more, and the other cyclists in the pack will appreciate it! If you've considered trying your hand at tandem racing, do it! By all accounts, tandem racing is about having fun. Racers say that the outstanding quality of tandem racing is the feeling of goodwill among the racers. They enjoy competing, and competing hard, but never at the expense of the other racers; no one has a career in tandem racing hanging on the line!

If racing sounds like fun, here are some tips and suggestions to help you get ready. First, choose your partner, and stick together. Choose someone who matches your riding style; not only your physical style but your level of interest in training, racing, and the importance you place on winning. The amount of experience you have together, and your commitment to your partnership, are probably the most important factors in your success (that is, your enjoyment of racing). Never blame each other in your disappointment; it doesn't help, and it takes all the fun out of tandem riding. Go out and ride like crazy. Practice turning and stopping in a parking lot to learn what your limits are on the tandem. You can get away with some things that you can't on a single, like hitting your pedals on the pavement while cornering. And there are some things you can't get away with, like scaring the wits out of the stoker! Work on pace line riding, and tandem handling in general—you owe it to the other riders in the race.

In the United States, tandem racing consists of the Burley Duet Stage Race (Eugene, Oregon), the Miami Valley Stage Race (Dayton, Ohio), a smattering of tandem criteriums in conjunction with well-established events, and sanctioned endurance races for all comers. Some of the sponsored U.S. teams, notably the Subaru-Montgomery team, have fielded tandems in the past, and if race promoters continue to see how exciting it is, tandem racing could become a more familiar sight.

The World Corporate Games have included tandem racing in the last few years, and may continue. Other than the Burley races, tandems are included as an aside, and an event which included a tandem race one year may or may not find room in the schedule the following year.

In Europe, tandem racing is better established; as many as forty tandems turn out for a weekend club tandem race. The club races are informal but well attended. A tandem stage race accompanied the Tour de France for three years in the 1980s. It attracted nearly one hundred teams, in spite of the requirement that the stoker be visually impaired. Tandem stage races are held throughout Europe each summer, and the level of competition is quite high.

Unfortunately, there is no master list of tandem races, so each one has to be searched out through various sponsoring organizations. The following contacts may help you find tandem races to participate in or watch.

For more information about tandem races which are sanctioned by the United States Cycling Federation (USCF), contact your local USCF representative or local racing club. The Tandem Club of America (see appendices for address) lists tandem races in their monthly newsletter.

For information about tandem races in Europe, contact Ray Patterson, PO Box 1081, Valley Center, CA, 92082-1081. He raced for a number of years in France, and because there is no "official" way to get information about European tandem racing, he generously offered to pass on what he can.

In the U.S., the Association for Blind Athletes (ABA) organizes tandem races as part of its schedule of events for athletes of various disciplines. The ABA focuses primarily on competition, and track and field events dominate the annual schedule. For more information contact ABA at 33 N. Institute, Colorado Springs, CO 80903 (719) 630-0422.

TOSRV Photo by Greg Siple

Tandem road racing in the United States is almost exclusively a Pacific Northwest phenomenon. This is due primarily to the efforts of the Burley Design Cooperative, makers of Burley Tandems. They promote the Burley Duet Classic, a six-stage race in early July each year which has a prize purse that puts it on par with major tandem events around the world. They also work with other promoters to organize a series of tandem races in the Northwest. For more information, contact the Burley Design Cooperative, 4080 Stewart Road, Eugene OR 97402 (503) 687-1644.

Tandem track racing is alive and well in the U.S., as is time trialing. Track racing is as fast as it gets—nothing beats the display of sheer power of tandems on the oval. Watching time trials (of any kind) takes a more practiced eye, or a more devoted fan, to really enjoy an afternoon sitting on the sidelines. It is much more interesting from the participant's point of view. Fortunately, it is the easiest type of racing for the otherwise non-racer because it places very few technical demands on the riders. Just get out there and go as fast as you can. Many local touring clubs hold informal weekly time trials which are open to all types of riders. For more information about tandem track racing and serious time trialing, contact your local USCF representative. Both riders must have current USCF licenses to participate in sanctioned races.

With more and more high-quality tandems on the market and with interest in tandems growing rapidly, tandem racing is sure to become a featured event at more and more races across the country. Keep an eye out for new tandem events!

Mountain Tandem Racing

Where there is a sport there is a race. Someone always wants to know how fast or how far they can go. Mountain tandem riders are no different. Well, actually, they are different, but you have to meet a few to know what we mean. They are expert bike handlers. And they are fearless. They like the speed of tandems, as we all do, but they also like the extra challenge of captaining a huge machine through the woods, or of holding on tight in the stoker's position, ready for anything, able to foresee nothing.

To describe the mountain tandem racing experience, without putting our own well-being at stake and actually doing it ourselves, we talked to Amy Wantulok, a five-year veteran of racing, and a tandem stoker in numerous mountain bike races. She says:

"The difference between road racing tandems and off-road racing is incredible. You really have to be in tune with the captain off-road—much more than on-road. There is a lot more you have to pay attention to when you're riding off-road. Both the captain and the stoker are basically out of the saddle the whole race. And when you're racing off-road, and you're the stoker, control of the bike is really out of your hands. You have to watch the captain's body for little clues; you can't pick them up from the road ahead. In road riding, you can see that a hill is coming up, or that the road curves, so you're ready when it happens. In off-road riding, you just have to hang on for dear life and be ready for anything and everything.

"People say you have to trust your captain, and that is true. But in off-road racing I have learned *not* to trust the captain. I have learned to say, 'I'm scared!' But really, I like going faster than on a single, and tandeming is great."

As more mountain tandems hit the dirt, more people will certainly join in the extreme test of tandem teamwork: mountain tandem racing.

Traveling with your Tandem

On the Car, or In It

You can't ride from your doorstep forever. You probably rode your single bikes from home for a while, but before long you had seen those same routes so often that you'd never want to ride them again. Those same last few miles to the house seem endless. It's time to load up and take the bikes out about thirty miles and go from there. You probably have the system down pretty well for carrying your single bikes on a car. But what do you do with that long tandem?

Angel designed the tandem attachment for the Yakima brand roof racks. The attachment goes on the rack without having to move the rack crossbars, so you can carry tandems and singles at the same time. The tandem attachments hold the front fork with a quick release, and the rear bottom bracket is secured to a special mount.

We almost always load the tandem together, though some people can do it single-handedly. It partly depends on how high the top of your car is, and partly on how strong you're feeling. For loading the bike on the roof of our van, we put the tandem mount as close to the outside of the rack as possible to make it easier to reach, and we step up on a cooler, box, or two-step ladder. If one of you is short and the car is high, you may have to have a step of some kind with you.

We drove a small car for a long time, and when it came time for a new vehicle, we chose a full-sized van so we could put the tandem inside. Now we don't worry about our leather saddles getting wet, or about squashed bugs on the head-tube and handlebars. We don't have to remove the bags or the cyclo-computer, and the wheels stay on, too.

The van doesn't have any back seats, and we built a bed that is easy to remove and replace. The bed is almost as wide as the van, but the tandem, or two mountain bikes, fit alongside. Then we drape the chains with a rag to protect the bedding. When we're camping, we sleep in the van, right next to the bike, and we know it's safe.

Tandem riders should consider a van when looking for a new car, especially if they want to drive with their tandem often. Even some of the smaller vans work, too. Take the tandem with you as you shop for a vehicle because it's as important as knowing if all the kids and the dog fit. To be polite to the car dealer, have the bike nice and clean, but be firm—you need to know whether the tandem is going to go in easily.

Tandem Boxes

Lots of people take their tandems on airplanes, buses, and trains. They go to Walla Walla, Wuhan, and Warsaw. People who use boxes either use the box that the tandem came in or get a commercially available tandem box. The advantages of using a tandem box are that the bike fits nicely, the box is sturdy, and if well-packed, the bike is protected. The disadvantages are that boxes are regularly abused by handlers who throw luggage around (we once saw a single bike in a box that had been dragged upright across the tarmac, and two inches of the bottom of the big chainring were ground off). In addition, you have to store the box somewhere while you are riding, and then return to it at the end of your trip.

Santana produces a large tandem box (over 30 pounds) used to ship new tandems to dealers. Both wheels remain in the frame and the wheels are suspended in the cartons internal cradles. Even if the box is dropped or dragged the wheels and tandem remain undamaged. Most Santana dealers save these "used once" boxes and sell them for $20 to $30. They're good for another trip or two.

Making Your Own Box

You can also rig up a box for a tandem out of two regular bike boxes, adding a little reinforcement. If you keep the box in this size: seventy inches long, 8.5 inches wide, and forty inches high, it will meet most airline bicycle-box standards. The advantages of this method are that it's inexpensive and you'll have fewer qualms about abandoning it and making another box later. If well-packed, your bike is protected. The disadvantages are that you have to do the box-making yourself, and the final product is probably not as sturdy as one integral box. And the bike might not fit as handily. Tandems will fit into the boxes supplied by most airlines (one where the single fits without removing either wheel) if you take off both wheels. In that situation, put the tandem in upside down, so the bike rests on the saddles, not the chainrings. Then put the wheels and accessories in another bike box, so that you have two normal (though large) bike boxes to deal with. It is also easier to avoid the word "tandem" at the ticket counter when you have two standard bike boxes. Many airlines have a special, higher rate for tandems; this two-box method lets you avoid the issue altogether. When they ask what's in the box simply say "a bicycle."

Tips on Storing the Box

At your destination, if you intend to use your box again, you will need to store the box for the duration of your ride.

The best option, obviously, is to leave it with family or friends. Another way is to take the tandem in the box to a bike shop, and pay a small fee for them to put the bike together and to store the box for the duration of the ride. Also, you could stay at a good hotel on your first and last nights, and arrange ahead of time for them to keep the box for you.

Going Without a Box

Some people send their tandem (or single) without a box. They take off the pedals, maybe turn the bars, and secure the moving parts. If you choose this method, pad anything you don't want scuffed. Tip: shift the derailleurs to the inside, so they are as close to the frame as possible, in the least vulnerable position. The advantages of this method are its simplicity. Nothing is likely to be stacked on top of it, and you don't have to find storage for a box, or come back to get a box. The disadvantages are that the paint could get scratched, the bike is not as well protected in the event it does get bumped around, and that not all carriers will take a bike that way.

Tandem Carrying Case

Nylon carrying cases for tandems are available. The advantages of a carrying case are that it is relatively permanent (it will not dissolve when left out on a wet tarmac), the bike fits very nicely, it has pockets for everything, and it is a bit more transportable than a box when the bike is not in it. The disadvantages are that you still have to store the case and come back for it at the end of the trip. The initial cost for this option is higher than the other options.

Shipping Your Tandem

Shipping the tandem ahead is the option we use most often while traveling inside the U.S. Send the bike in a box through a shipping company a week or ten days before you go on your trip. If you send it to a shop (which you had previously contacted), you can have your tandem ready to ride when you arrive. They may also store the box for you while you are riding, and ship the tandem home for you when you are finished. The advantages are that you don't have to drag the tandem around several airports with you, you don't have to transport it from the airport to where you start riding, and shipping companies are simply better handlers than airline baggage employees; if you write "This Side Up" and "Do Not Stack," it is much more likely to be heeded than on the airlines. The disadvantages are that you need a mailing address at your destination with someone to accept the tandem during working hours, you are without your tandem the week before the ride while it is being shipped, and shipping costs are a little higher than most airline fees.

Airplanes

There are two schools of thought about taking tandems on airliners. We'll share the method we've used first. Our personal advice when flying with any bicycle is to call ahead. Find out what the policy is of the airline you're traveling on. Both Northwest and American Airlines recognize a tandem bicycle as a checkable item, as may some others. Ask your travel agent to book you only on planes that are at least as big as a DC-9 or 737. The tandem box just doesn't fit into the cargo holds of a regional commuter plane.

Then we check on the size restrictions, making it clear that the bike is big. Ask who you're speaking with, and make a note of it. If you felt the person wasn't sure (or if you didn't like the answer!), call again, and talk to someone else. You might even shop for an airline with your tandem needs in mind. Once you have agreed with someone about how the bike should be packed, then do your best to pack it that way.

The second method, untested by us, has been used exclusively by Bill McCready who often takes 4–5 Santana tandems with him to trade shows and tandem rallies. His instructions? "Don't ask—don't tell." After buying his tickets from a travel agent he simply shows up very early for his flight—at least two hours before departure. We'll let him tell the rest ... "I usually drag the tandem boxes into the terminal while my wife Jan parks the car. I then leave the boxes off to one side while I make my way through the check-in line. After checking our suitcases and re-verifying the seat assignments I pull out my credit card and say, 'Oh, and I need to pay for the bikes.' Eighty percent of the time, even when I have a half-dozen boxed tandems, they simply fill out the forms and take my money. If they remark on the size I'll tell them, 'I'm sure it's fine—I've done this many times before.' I know for a fact Santana's standard cartons (100″ × 10″ × 40″) will fit through the cargo doors of every jetliner in commercial service—my record is seven of these big boxes in a rather small 737. If someone at the counter asks why the boxes are so big I tell them it's because the bikes are expensive and the larger size allows more padding and better protection (all true). I don't confuse them by telling them the bike has extra seats.

"In a very few instances, less than one time in twenty, the person behind the counter balks. This is why I've shown up early and purchased my tickets through a travel agent. At this point I'll tell them the arrangements to bring the boxed bikes were all confirmed by my travel agent when she booked the ticket. Actually, I used to have my travel agent do this and no longer bother. If they still resist I'll helpfully suggest they look in their computer 'I'm sure it's in there someplace.' If they are still resistant, I'll tell them 'I think the travel agent told me there is something written on the ticket' and ask them to explain the coded gibberish. Only twice in twenty years have I had to resort to asking to speak to the manager. I then calmly go through all these same steps a second time. Only once have I had to resort to a mild threat, something like, 'If the bikes don't go, I won't go either,' (absolutely true). 'I hate to think I'm going to have to cancel my entire trip and request refunds from hotels because you can't find my travel agent's instructions in your computer'. Because I've shown up early and stayed completely calm, I have a perfect record of never missing a flight or leaving a tandem behind.

"Further, I've shared my method with dozens of tandems owners who have called me after phoning the airlines and getting the run-around. In every case I've asked them to report back to me if they miss their flight—no one has ever reported a failure."

Buses

As with airlines, check ahead for rules on bus lines in your area. Most big buses have a cargo hold big enough, but that doesn't mean they have room on every run. Try to make a luggage space reservation. Is it okay if your bike goes on an earlier or later bus? If you give them a little flexibility, it could make a difference as to whether or not they want to deal with your tandem. Do they have a freight service? Does it have different policies? Be sure to check costs. Again, don't mention that the bike is a tandem, but tell them the dimensions of the box to make sure they can accommodate it.

Trains

Trains throughout Europe and Canada will take a tandem without a box. They often allow you to load it yourself. Unfortunately, Amtrak has a stated no-tandem policy. However, they allow the largest bicycle box; the kind a single fits into without taking off the wheels. Put your tandem in one or two (tandem without wheels in the first, wheels and other accessories in the other) of those boxes and just label them "bicycles." We know it sounds a little sneaky, but the fact that the machine in the box has two seats instead of one should not interest them if they accept bicycles at all. It is simply a discriminatory policy.

Make sure to call ahead. We have heard a variety of reports over the years about Amtrak policies regarding single bicycles which vary from city to city. Rules are likely to be different depending on the locale. Sometimes Amtrak requires boxes, sometimes they require that you use their boxes, and in one case, they required that we use their box, but they didn't have any.

General

Traveling *with* a bike is a lot like traveling *on* a bike. Either process is not entirely predictable. In both cases we've learned that flexibility, determination and a calm smile will win the day—even when you can't speak the language. You *can* take a tandem with you!

Louis & Julie Melini, with Benjamin (4) & Carlo (2). Salt Lake City, Utah

Day riding in Montana and Idaho

(They all wear helmets which were left out in the confusion of photo taking.)

"We found with one child that we could do 40–60 miles a day comfortably, allowing time for our child to have his time to play. He slept about one third of the time in the trailer so a small pillow was helpful. Also we put pillows below his feet so that he wouldn't slide down the seat after a few bumps. One good part of bicycling with a trailer is the room cars give you. I suppose that it's okay to injure adults on bikes but not kids."

Greg & Zane Siple Missoula, Montana

Greg Siple and his son Zane, age 6, show off their Burley Duet that has been turned into a fish. The two had just ridden the modified bike in the parade that kicks off the International Wildlife Film Festival in Missoula, Montana. Zane had recently graduated from a trailer to the 'kidback' equipped tandem.

How to Choose a Tandem

MANY PEOPLE who are shopping for tandems are justifiably excited and nervous at the same time. They're excited because they anticipate owning a tandem, and they're nervous because it is probably the third most expensive purchase they've ever made. The house is the most costly, the car is second, and then the tandem. It has to be just right.

How can you be sure that you are going to get the tandem of your dreams, without having nightmares in the process? Here are our suggestions for choosing a tandem—how to enjoy the process and come out with the tandem that fits your needs and your pocketbook.

When you decide to buy a tandem:
1. Choose a bike shop you trust and which inspires your confidence.
2. Know what you are going to use the tandem for.
3. Know what to look for in a tandem.
4. Talk to tandem owners.

Choosing a Shop

The most important choice you can make when you decide to buy a tandem is choosing the right bike shop. You need to find a shop that caters to tandem customers. It is important

Attending a tandem rally can gain vital feedback from tandem enthusiasts.

that they are able to help select the right tandem for you, that they can answer all of your questions and concerns, and that they can continue to offer a high level of service after you have bought the bike.

The shop you deal with should have resident experts who really know tandems. That person is usually a tandem enthusiast, and has experience riding as well as selling and servicing tandems. The fact that a shop has a person who is considered the specialist means that they take tandeming seriously. This is a prime consideration, and you will appreciate your ability to rely on this person for product information as well as service expertise.

Try to find a shop in your area that has several tandems displayed on the floor and specializes in tandems. Ask the dealer if he or one of his staff rides tandems, and talk to the tandem expert in the shop. Ask him how long the shop has been selling tandems. You can get an idea of their level of commitment in just a few minutes. If you don't have a shop in your area that is tandem-oriented, go to the shop you normally do business with. Tell them you are interested in buying a tandem, and rely on their experience and contacts to secure the tandem and accessories you're looking for. A good working relationship with your local bike shop will save you time and money as you maintain and improve your tandem.

If you find that your local shop is not tandem-oriented, and doesn't inspire your confidence enough for you to place a special order with them for a tandem, consider making a special trip to a shop outside of your immediate area that does specialize in tandems. Before you go, be sure to call ahead to see if they have a variety of tandems, and will be able to help you with your needs. Make an appointment so you can have the tandem specialist's full attention.

All else failing, you can get good service through the mail from one of the half dozen dealers nationwide that specialize in tandems. These dealers have lots of experience in selling through the mail, and will send you information and take the time to make sure that you get the bike you want and need.

In the appendices we have listed some of the shops which specialize in tandems. Not all shops—not even all the good ones—know very much about tandems. It takes a commitment from the owners and managers to cater specifically to tandem riders. It is very difficult to get good information about tandems, and that is one of the reasons we wrote this book.

Buying a Custom Tandem

If you have decided to order a custom tandem, be sure to ask the builder a lot of questions. Many builders who make just a few bikes a year make even fewer tandems. Be sure that the custom shop you choose has some experience and interest in tandems. Ask them for references from some of their past tandem customers. Ask what their building philosophy is.

We have too often seen custom tandems from small builders that are barely workable, or are more a reflection of the builder than of the riders. The tandem was designed to be the dream bike for the builder (who is a racer or fast sport rider for example) instead of the perfect bike for the riders (who are tourists). Building the right tandem for particular riders involves much more than putting tubes together at the correct angles. Many small builders don't even have the proper tube selection for the frame and fork, or have not made enough tandems to have worked out the bugs in the assembly process. A tandem builder has to make at least a dozen tandems a year to really be called a tandem builder.

Once you have chosen the shop which is going to fit your needs, you have to choose the right tandem.

What are You Going to Use it For?

It's the same question you asked yourself when you were choosing a single bike. Day riding? Overnight touring? Racing and time trialing? Off-road riding? You probably enjoy more than one kind of riding, and most tandems perform well in more than one related specialty. Choose the function and features that are most important to you. You can have a tandem that is designed for light touring and performs in the club time trial equally well; but you'd better not try to get a racing tandem which you can later use to ride around the world.

In general, most tandem purchasers know what kind of tandem they want. Many new buyers have been cyclists for some time, and have already defined their riding styles. The most popular styles are sport and touring, with mountain tandems becoming more popular all the time. The following discussion of tandem uses will help you match your riding style with the features which will serve you the best.

Sport

Sport riding is essentially unloaded riding where speed is important. It encompasses casual time trials, day riding, and supported multi-day riding (as opposed to fully-loaded touring). The gearing is a bit higher than touring bikes and overall light weight is a consideration. These bikes usually have 700c rims with 1" or 1⅛" tires. The geometry's are direct lateral and marathon.

Touring

Touring tandems can be subdivided into light touring or full touring, but the bike is basically the same. Full touring involves multi-day trips where the tandem team is fully self-sufficient, carrying all their gear for camping. Light tourists stay indoors overnight, and are not carrying bedding or cooking utensils. The gears are generally lower than for sport riding, allowing easier climbing. This tandem can have as many as seven or eight bottle cages. It has full braze-ons for front and rear racks and fenders. If the wheels are 27" or 700c they have 1⅛" or 1¼" tires. Or they are 26", and have 1.25" to 1.9" tires; the smaller wheels are stronger and accept a wider variety of tires. The geometry's are usually direct lateral or double diamond. (See Chapter 9 for discussion of frame geometries)

Racing

Pure-bred racing tandems are rare since tandem racing is itself rare. The most specialized of the racing tandems are the track tandems. Just like other track bikes, they have one gear and no brakes. Years ago, tandem track racing was an Olympic event, and many more track tandems were manufactured. Now tandem events are picking up at track races, but until it is an Olympic sport again, tandem track bikes won't be made in great numbers. Racing tandems have tight frame geometry's (putting the riders close together in aerodynamic positions), usually direct internal or marathon design. Racing tandems have light wheels, and road racing tandems have high gears.

Mountain

Mountain bike tandems are just like singles; they are made to go off the pavement. They are characterized by fat, knobby tires, low gears, and upright handlebars. They are often used for both on- and off-road riding. If you plan to use one for long road rides you might consider drop bars and smaller tires.

Casual

Casual and recreational tandems are the one-three-, and five-speeds that are often rented at resorts. Usually the geometry is men's/mixte or mixte/mixte. These tandems are not often used for serious road riding, but they are a lot of fun, and we have seen them on tours in flat areas of the Midwest.

Counterpoint Tandems

A Counterpoint tandem is totally different from traditional tandems. It is a combination of a regular bike and a recumbent, and the captain and stoker have independent control of their cadences. The captain rides in the back on what looks like a conventional bike, and controls the steering and basic gear selection. The stoker rides in front in a recumbent position, pedaling a crank that is out on a boom in front of the seat. The stoker can choose a different cadence by using an independent freewheel, which allows variation in relation to the primary gear. The stoker can also coast while the captain continues pedaling.

The old joke about the Counterpoint tandem is that it looks like a man on a unicycle pushing a woman in a wheelbarrow. Jokes aside, the Counterpoint is a very elegant solution for many tandemists. Both the captain and the stoker have an excellent view of the road ahead, each of them has control over the cadence they choose to ride in, and the recumbent seat is essential for some folks who can't, or don't want to sit on a regular bike seat. All in all, Jim Weaver's Counterpoint is one of those ideas that I wish I had thought of.

We have ridden many miles next to Counterpoint tandems. They go just as fast and are just as social as any tandem. Unfortunately, Counterpoints are sold in only one shop, in the Seattle area, so you might have a hard time test riding one. Your best bet is to attend the Northwest Tandem Rally on Memorial Day weekend where they are always well represented.

Recumbent tandems are increasingly popular.

Other kinds of tandems

At various tandem rallies we have seen just about every kind of bicycle that can be ridden by two people. We have seen double recumbents that look like two single recumbents stuck together, both facing forward. Then there's the two recumbents that are joined back to back. How about a single recumbent of gigantic proportions, twenty feet long, with both riders on one long boom. Backyard builders have a field day inventing and building tandems. Many of them are very rideable, and they are all certainly conversation pieces. Many more highly-functional designs are being offered as technology progresses.

Talk to Tandem Owners

A good way to get a lot of user information is to attend one of the tandem rallies held all over the U.S. each summer (See the appendices for more information). It is not uncommon for riders to attend on single bikes, and ask lots of questions. Tandem owners love to talk about their bikes, and their experiences in buying and riding their tandems are invaluable. You might also contact a tandem club near you (again, check the appendices) and go on one of their day rides. It's another great way to talk to lots of tandem riders and learn how they pursue their sport.

Take one precaution in talking to tandem owners: they have invested a lot of money in their tandem, and they are going to say good things about it. Once they've made the investment, they have to like it! In my experience, most tandem owners are very happy with their bikes, even when it is obvious that it isn't the right bike for them. This is especially true of custom bikes. Many of our customers at R&E Bicycles are very happy with a bike we made many years ago, which is nowhere near as good as what we're making now. Angel actually knew very little about making tandems when he started building them fifteen years ago. He learns a little more on every ride and at every tandem rally.

Why Tandems are Expensive

Countless times people have come into a retail store to discuss buying a tandem, and were shocked speechless when the price came up. Most tandem riders have had the experience of discussing tandeming with a passerby at a cafe or park who asks, "So, what does a machine like that cost?" They are usually flabbergasted by the reply, and say something like, "I could buy a motorcycle, or even a car, for that much!"

Why are tandems so seemingly expensive? Why should they cost so much more than two single bikes of the same quality?

The answer is apparent when you look at the numbers. We estimate there are approximately five thousand to six thousand high quality (more than $1,000) tandems sold in the U.S. each year. When you compare that to the nine to eleven million bikes made and sold each year, you realize that tandems represent a very small segment of the overall bicycle market. For the most part, each tandem is hand-crafted or made in small production batches. Manufacturers who make millions of components find it a bother to make a small run of special hubs or cranks. When pressed, these companies admit they do it as a marketing tactic or for the prestige of offering a full line of components. Tandems are expensive because so few are made.

Another reason that tandems are expensive is that they must use the best of everything. The stresses that a tandem has to withstand are much greater than what a single bike has to endure. A single bike manufacturer can use any one of a variety of components. Tandem makers must use only high quality components. If you made a single bike with components that met basic tandem standards, it would to cost more than $1,000.

Choosing the Right Size Tandem

Sizing rules are generalizations with lots of exceptions. In general, stock tandems fit teams with a height difference of three to eight inches. A difference of more than eight, or less than three inches, can be optimized with a custom tandem. If you want to be able to trade off captaining and stoking, a height difference of four inches and a weight difference of twenty percent is ideal.

Having said all that, I have made many tandems for teams where the captain was significantly smaller than the stoker. One in particular had a captain who was five-foot-three and a stoker close to six feet, with a weight difference much greater than 20 percent. The top tube sloped from back to front, making the tandem quite a unique-looking machine. The sighted captain and her blind husband stoker enjoy the tandem tremendously.

Tandem top tubes usually slope down from front to back. Because of that, the head tube is higher compared to the same size single bike, and the captain's position is slightly different. A single road bike's top tube is level with the ground, and when the seat is the right height, the handlebars are at about the right place for a comfortable riding position. If you select the captain's end of the tandem by the length of the seat tube, you end up with a head tube that is higher than that of a single road bike. That is usually okay because most captains like a bit shorter top tube and stem combination, and a bit higher handlebar position, than they do on a single.

For the stoker, the most important size consideration is that the top tube be plenty long. The longer rear top tube allows for better comfort and gives the stoker ample distance from the captain's back. The stoker's top tube height and seat tube length is not as important on a tandem as on a single because the stoker does not have to handle the bike. If the seat and handlebars are in the right position, it doesn't matter very much what the tube sizes are under the stoker.

If you have to compromise between perfect fit for the captain and for the stoker—most tandem fits are at least a bit of compromise—choose a captain's seat tube that is on the small side. Remember that the stoker's handlebars are attached to the captain's seatpost. If the captain's seat tube is too long, and the seatpost rises only slightly out of the frame, there is no room on the seatpost to adjust the height of the rear bars. There will also be less space between the captain's thighs and the stoker's hands on the bars. Riding with your thighs touching the stoker's bars on each pedal stroke annoys you and the stoker. For the stoker's end of the tandem, if you're making compromises, it is acceptable for the rear top tube to be too high. You can use the mount and dismount technique that allows the stoker to get on and off while the captain supports the tandem.

A Ryan Recumbent Tandem.

Stock tandems are made in carefully selected standard sizes, and most couples fit one of them. To fine-tune each rider's fit, you adjust the stem and the seatpost. Most teams can use a stock bike.

But fit alone is not the only reason to get a custom tandem. A custom tandem is built to fit you and your riding partner exactly. Each tube is sized to your body's proportions for a perfect fit and unsurpassed comfort. A custom tandem is also designed for your particular riding style and intended use. Every detail is addressed with you and your riding partner in mind. Best of all, you decide what goes on the tandem: braze-ons, components, and the paint. Of course, you must pay for it all, but we think it's worth it.

A couple who had been married for seventeen years pulled me aside and told me that their custom tandem was the second largest purchase they had ever made, and that they had been contemplating the new tandem for a long time. A few months latter they dropped by to tell me that they were sorry that they had waited so long before getting their tandem.

The last word on fit is: if it's comfortable for you, it fits. And whatever you have to do to make it fit is okay. We make a point of noticing interesting stoker handlebar arrangements. The variety is infinite, and every arrangement is one hundred percent right. The magazine photos of perfectly dressed, trim, fit young couples on tandems are misleading. Tandem teams come in all sizes and shapes, and in all levels of fitness. Their tandems fit their needs, rather than the needs of fashion photographers. Attend any tandem rally, and you'll see what we mean when we say that when it comes to comfort, anything goes!

Mike, Marge, Caitlin and John Powers

Minneapolis, Minnesota

Tandeming around Missoula

Mike, a lab technician, his wife Marge, a mortician, and their 2 children, Caitlin and John, were in Missoula for a wedding and decided to buy a Santana tandem with a trailer. Next thing they knew they were on the road as one happy family.

Cindy and Tim Dellett-Wion

Bridgewater, Virginia

Anacortes, Washington to Yorktown, Virginia

There is a mystical quality about being on the road. There are no rules. You leave everything behind and embark on a truly life-changing experience. The change in your life lies on the roads ahead. Touring gets into your psyche and there will undoubtedly be many more adventures for us in the future.

Setting Up the Tandem

Gearing

Gearing is one of the subjects that tandemists (and all bicyclists) debate as an on-going recreational activity. That means that there are a variety of opinions out there, and we'll add ours here.

A tandem team should choose gearing that is a tiny bit higher than what the stronger of the two riders uses on a single bike. Now and then we see tandems with huge sixty-tooth front chainrings, and the riders tell us how they spin out a 56×12-tooth cog regularly. But those teams are the exception, and we sometimes suspect that they're stretching things a bit.

Every now and then we could use a bigger gear, especially on a long, moderate, downhill run, but not too often. We are usually going fast enough downhill. At the beginning of the season we start out with 50/42/28 tooth chainrings on our front triple. As we become stronger, we change to a 52/44/28, and by the end of the season we're at 54/44/28. Our rear cog set is generally 13/14/16/18/20/24/28.

We think of our gears as if we had three seven-speed bikes. Most of the time we're in our middle range seven-speed; down hill or with a stiff breeze at our backs, we use our high range seven-speed and on the uphill we use our lowest chainring and the three or four biggest cogs. Angel doesn't try to shift between chainrings to find the next higher gear in the sequence (he says can't keep track of half-step shifting, a method that has the rider shift once on the front and once on the rear, thereby getting an even progression of steps). Most of the time we want to keep it simple, and quite often we will make five or six shifts within a thirty second period as we start up a hill.

When riders talk about gears, terms like fifteenth gear or fifth gear are meaningless. The only way to talk about gearing is in terms of gear ratios. To calculate the gear ratio for any combination of wheels and gears, do the following. Divide the number of teeth on the front chainring by the number of teeth on the rear cog, and multiply by the diameter of your wheel in inches. For example, if your chainring is 52 and the rear cog you're using is a 14, and your wheel is 27 inches in diameter, then you're in 100-inch gear. My 100-inch gear is the same as your 100-inch gear even if we have different chainrings, cogs, and wheels.

Take a few minutes to count the teeth on your chainrings and cogs and measure your wheel diameter (measure your own to get an accurate figure for your particular wheel and tire combination) and make yourself a chart of the progression of your gears. If you want to explore more about gearing, there is at least one whole book dedicated to the subject.

Phasing

As long as you maintain an active interest in tandems you will hear talk about the pros and cons of different phasings. Phasing is how the captain's and stoker's cranks are set in relation to each other. The crossover chain which connects the two sets of cranks (the arms that support the pedals) can be loosened, allowing the pedals to be positioned in relation to each other. Most tandems are arranged with the two sets of cranks together: that is, both riders have their right feet up at the same time.

However, there is more than one way to arrange tandem pedals. Tandem cranks can be arranged in two functional ways: "in-phase" or "out-of-phase." In-phase means that both the front and rear cranks are set in the same relation; when the captain's cranks are at twelve and six o'clock, so are the stoker's. Out-of-phase is when the captain's cranks are at twelve and six o'clock, and the stoker's cranks are ninety degrees off, pointing to nine and three o'clock. Out-of-phase actually refers to any position that does not exactly match the two riders' pedals

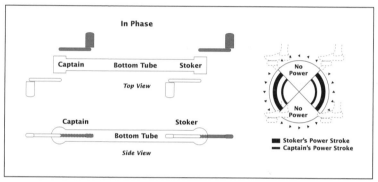

We have ridden both ways, and for the last few years have preferred to ride very slightly out-of-phase, in an arrangement which Jack Goertz of Tandems Ltd. so kindly calls the "Rodriguez Timing Overlap." We'll go into that more a bit later in this section.

When we started tandeming in the late 1970s, almost everyone rode in-phase. The tandem frames in those days were generally not as strong in respect to side-to-side motion, and probably could not have supported the additional stress of riding out-of-phase. Riding in-phase is the easiest way to start out on a tandem. From the beginning, getting on and off is easier, as is starting from intersections (especially if both riders put a foot down). The riders have a tremendous feeling of togetherness right from the start; the tandem moves with the riders, and it's easy to get a rhythm going. It is also easier for the riding partners to overlook the differences in pedaling style and in power, since both riders are pushing on the pedals at the same time. Riding in-phase certainly looks more like tandeming than does riding out-of-phase. It's one of the reasons that we are now back in-phase, as are a lot of other people. It just looks better.

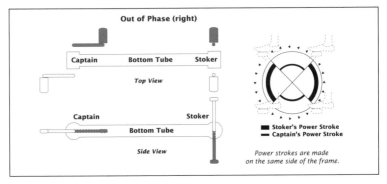

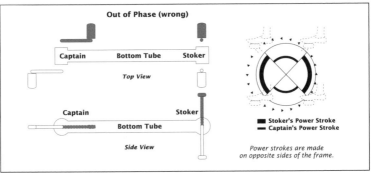

Riding out-of-phase has an advantage which lured us from in-phase between 1981 and 1985. The power is continuous: one partner is always in a power position, filling the gap when the other is near the twelve o'clock and 6 o'clock position (the "dead spot" where it is impossible to apply much power). The smooth ride is particularly noticeable when you're climbing at a low cadence. Conversely, it takes more practice to spin at a normal cadence out-of-phase. We have a fairly high cadence, and we know that there is a difference in power between us. If that sounds like your style, then out-of-phase could suit you.

The power difference comes into play when one person is pushing considerably harder, giving the tandem a slight, lurching feel. However, when we were at cruising speed at a high cadence, neither of us could feel the difference in power.

We found out-of-phase more continuous, from the speed and power points of view. On hills with a gentle rise, (less than four percent) we found that we lost hardly any speed, and we certainly didn't get the feeling that we were grinding along, like we sometimes do in-phase. Both riders must be quite smooth in their pedaling and upper body motions.

There is another advantage to out-of-phase from the point of view of wear and tear on the components of the tandem. The forces on the bottom brackets are reduced by nearly half that of riding in-phase. In-phase subjects both of the chains to much more stress. It also increases the stress on the wheels and shifting system.

We remember clearly the very first time we rode out-of-phase. We had been talking about changing over for weeks but we weren't convinced, and Carla was rather opposed to the idea. We thought that it wouldn't work and that we would never be able to stand up together; something we enjoyed quite a bit and took pride in. One day without telling Carla, I changed the phasing just before our regular Saturday morning club ride. I planned to mount and dismount while leaning against something, so Carla wouldn't notice the unusual pedal positions, since we usually both put a foot down.

For the first five miles, she was complaining about my wiggling, and would I please keep still and concentrate on my riding. When we came to a hill where we always stood up, she said, "Well, let's stand up." I figured that we might as well try it. When we stood up she could see clearly that we were out-of-phase and all she could do was laugh. So did everyone else in the group; they all knew of my experiment. After we both knew that we were out-of-phase, things got much smoother. And we knew we could stand up.

There are two ways to set a tandem out-of-phase. One works well and the other works quite badly. We suspect that many riders who say, "I tried out-of-phase and hated it," have good reason to say so! Riding out-of-phase the wrong way has resulted in some of the oddest tandeming we've done; wiggling down the road, unable to ride smoothly or in a straight line. The correct way to set the cranks out-of-phase puts the stoker's pedal stroke following the captain's (the opposite is the wrong way: to have the stoker's right-side power stroke follow the captain's left-side power stroke).

To arrange the cranks out-of-phase correctly, set the captain's right pedal at twelve o'clock, poised for the power stroke. Then set the stoker's right pedal at nine o'clock (or better, a little closer to the captain's pedal, at about eighty degrees), to follow with another power stroke on the same side.

Everyone, even the smoothest of riders, leans a little bit towards the leg which is pushing at the moment; that lean affects the steering of the bicycle. When the captain of a tandem leans, he steers the tandem just a little to compensate. The correct out-of-phase arrangement, described above, allows the power lean of the stoker to follow the captain's lean, (and therefore the tandem's lean). If the out-of-phase arrangement is wrong, the captain's lean and steering comes after the stoker's lean, and the two riders are working against each other. We've seen teams who looked like ungainly caterpillars wiggling down the road because their tandems are out-of-phase wrong.

Starting from a stop when each rider has a foot on the ground is probably the most difficult out-of-phase maneuver. The way we do it, and teach others to, is to have the captain put his right foot between four and five o'clock, which puts the stoker's right foot between one and two o'clock. The captain has a bit of power to help him get on the saddle, then the stoker has to keep the bike moving. The other option is for the stoker to get on first, before you go anywhere. Then the captain can put his pedal anywhere he chooses, and the stoker is ready for the first power stroke. At stops, the stoker stays on, being careful not to lean.

It takes some skill for both riders to stand up at the same time when the pedals are out-of-phase. It is possible, and not too difficult, if you are good at standing up in-phase. If riding out of the saddle is one of your goals, start by standing one at a time, and becoming comfortable with that. Then try getting out of the saddle at the same time, on the signal of the captain. Be ready to sit if the tandem feels unstable. We find that rising to the standing position at the same time is the most effective, but you may find that having one or the other of you up first is easier. Just keep working at it because it is possible!

Some tandem teams say that cornering is more dangerous out-of-phase. However, if you look at the pedal positions, you see that when the captain corners the tandem with his inside foot up, as on a single, the stoker's pedal position is nine and three o'clock, certainly not close to the ground. When teams finally master riding out-of-phase, many never go back to riding in-phase.

We presently ride slightly out-of-phase, so slightly that many experienced tandem teams don't even notice. It's what Jack Goertz calls the "Rodriguez Timing Overlap." What got us to ride in-phase after several fun and strong years out-of-phase were Shimano Bio-Pace chainrings. These are oval chainrings

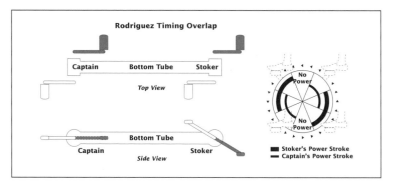

Rodriguez Timing Overlap

Captain   Bottom Tube   Stoker

Top View

Bottom Tube

Captain   Stoker

Side View

No Power

No Power

■ Stoker's Power Stroke
— Captain's Power Stroke

which promised to make better mechanical use of your pedal stroke. When they came out we just had to try them, and the only way that it made any sense was in-phase. So we switched. We finally moved away from the Bio-Pace chainrings on the outer two rings, but we decided to stay in-phase It just looks better and feels more together.

But we missed the more continuous power of out-of-phase, and began experimenting with being just slightly out-of-phase. Now we're just a few links out, about ten degrees. It works just fine for us; it looks just as good as in-phase, but extends our power stroke by a considerable percentage. Even this slight overlap must be arranged with the stoker cranks following, as described for full out-of-phase.

Strong tandem teams, like racers and cross-country record teams, seem to prefer in-phase. In short races where there is a pack of tandems riding shoulder to shoulder, split-second timing is important, and being in-phase helps the tandem team make its moves. We once asked Rob Templin and Pete Penseyers, cross-USA tandem champions, why they made their record cross country ride in-phase. They just shrugged their shoulders and said that they had tried it both ways, and that riding with both of them out of the saddle was easier.

Remember, changing the phasing of your tandem is easy; it takes only a few minutes. If you want to do some experimenting, which we suggest you do, go out for an easy ride and leave the crossover chain loose enough to take off the crossover rings by hand. Try lots of combinations, and when you find something you like, adjust the tension of the crossover chain again. Remember not to ride too hard with the chain loose; it can come off.

Give different phasing a fair chance by tightening up the crossover, and going all day on one which you think you might like. Like any change on the tandem, you'll need some time to adjust to the new feel before you can really make a judgment.

Timing Chains and Tandem Drive Arrangements

Timing chains are common to all traditional tandems. The non-traditional tandems which don't have timing chains are the older side-by-sides, the current Counterpoints, and other recumbent or semi-recumbent tandems. The timing chain ties the front crank and the rear crank together on a secondary set of chainrings so that they turn at same rate. The timing chain allows both riders to provide power to the drive chain. The drive chain is the one that goes to the rear wheel, propelling the tandem.

The timing chain might more appropriately be called the "captain's power transfer chain" since that is what it really does: when the captain rides the tandem alone, the timing chain turns the stoker's crank, which then turns the drive chain. The cranks can be in any phase (see the Phasing section) but they will always turn at the same rate.

Among the unique components on a tandem are the cranks and their accompanying hardware. Often, experienced cyclists as well as non-cyclists ask how tandemists pedal so perfectly in unison. And it is sometimes hard to convince folks that tandem teams with their pedals out-of-phase are pedaling at the same cadence. The secret is the timing chain.

The size of the timing chainrings varies from tandem to tandem. It used to be that most tandems used TA brand cranks. TA supplied special crossover chainrings with their cranks, and those chainring sizes happened to be 32 or 36 teeth. For many years most tandems had small timing chainrings for that reason alone. Now most experts feel that larger crossover chainrings are better: they wear much longer, and put less stress on the bottom bracket bearings. The only drawback is that larger chainrings need a longer chain, and therefore add a little bit of weight. But most riders are happy to take the extra weight in exchange for the longer life of the chain, chainrings, and bottom bracket.

Timing chainrings on the same tandem can be different sizes, though it is not common. It is set up in the case of a child stoker who can't keep up with the captain's cadence; the child's chainring is larger than the captain's chainring. Then the stoker's feet go around more slowly than the captain's. This isn't a solution for two adults who don't agree on cadence, however. The phasing constantly changes as the cranks turn, and with the power and weight of an adult, the tandem would never handle or perform well.

There are two basic types of tandem crank arrangements: crossover drives, in which the timing chain is on the left side of the bike, and side drives, in which both chains are on the right side of the tandem. Even though crossover drives are almost universal today, a discussion of the other drives is in order, as well as why someone might consider using them.

Crossover Drives

Tandems with crossover drives have the timing chain on the left and the drive chain on the right. There are two configurations: the crossover rear drive, and the crossover front drive.

The crossover rear drive is the most common crank arrangement, and it is used on most modern tandems. The timing chain is on the left, and the drive chain runs between the rear cranks and the rear wheel. The captain has a single chainring on the left and a plain crank on the right. The stoker has a shoelace-devouring single chainring on the left and a normal triple chainring crank on the right. Specially-drilled and tapped cranksets are needed for this configuration. The cranks are different from singles because you need to have left cranks that accept chainrings, and one plain right crank arm.

The crossover front drive configuration has the timing chain on the left and the drive crank on the captain's right side, with a very long chain running to the rear wheel. It is only used in some kidback conversions, and by my friend John Allen.

Side Drives

Side drives, which have the timing chain on the same side as the drive chain, come in two configurations: the rear side drive and the front side drive. They are not used anymore by any of the major tandem makers. The main advantages are that normally threaded crank sets can be used instead of having to use special tandem cranks, and that they put less load on the bottom bracket bearings. The major disadvantage is that one of the drive chainrings is lost to the timing function, leaving only two for power. Almost every tandem needs three chainrings.

Rear side drives have the timing chain on the right side, and the drive chain goes from rear cranks to the rear wheel. Most of the first rideable tandems, produced in the 1890s, used a rear side drive. Early tandems also had only one rear cog, so that chain alignment was easy: there was no problem of chain deflection angle as with multi-cog freewheels. Now you see this arrangement only on track tandems.

Front side drives have the timing chain on the right, and a very long drive chain between the front cranks and the rear wheel. As wide-space, multi-cog rear clusters came into use thirty years ago, builders quickly discovered the shifting limitations of short chainstays. They produced bad chain angles on the gear extremes. Derailleurs didn't shift well, and chains wore out quickly. The simple solution on a tandem was to have the driving crank on the front of the bike, connected to the freewheel with a long chain. This virtually eliminated the chain angle problem. The drawback was that the bike had a lot of chain which was heavy, and the rear derailleur had a hard time handling that much chain.

Norm and Vee Drexel

New Zealand

Calgary, Canada to Jackson, Wyoming

Norm and Vee Drexel used their Santana tandem to escape the winter in New Zealand where they operate an "American style breakfast and lunch restaurant" in Christchurch. They cycled from Calgary in Canada to Jackson, Wyoming. Though they made their tour in July they still ran into bits of northern hemisphere winter in the higher altitudes of the Rocky Mountains.

Tandem Systems and Components

THE QUALITY OF a tandem is largely determined by the quality of its parts. Every manufacturer selects each component of a tandem carefully. They have to balance function, cosmetics, and cost for each model and price range. And every custom tandem buyer has to do the same thing. Every nut, bolt, and washer plays a role on the tandem, and each should be chosen with care and thought. Anyone upgrading a tandem goes through the same process.

This discussion of components is intended to help the team who is considering buying a custom tandem. A tandem is a big investment, but the difference in price between a custom tandem and a stock tandem is not all that big. Even when a team is a perfect fit for an off-the-shelf tandem, there is a certain pride of ownership and expression that can only be achieved by having a unique, "this was made for us" tandem.

A review of each component and its function will help you decide how to maximize performance and appearance for your money. Some people only consider function, but to others, looks are just as important. You could spend a lot of time and money upgrading non-essential components, and not notice the difference in comfort or performance. If you're considering upgrading, look at the components in the order they appear in this chapter. We have organized the chapter according to the importance each part plays in the comfort and quality of ride.

If you are really interested in reading about and comparing hardware, we recommend *Upgrading Your Bike*, by Frank Berto, Rodale Press, 1988. Any book about parts is a bit out of date as it relates to specific parts, but Berto's comparisons and basic insights are still quite sound.

Frames and Forks

Because I have been in the frame building business for many years, my first temptation is to launch into a long, technical discussion of tandem geometry's and frame-building techniques. But I won't do that here. I will, however, present an overview of tandem frame terminology and geometry's.

All "traditional" tandem frame designs share the tubes of the open frame design. The other frame designs are elaboration's on the basic open frame design.

Open Frame. The most basic tandem design is the open frame. An open frame is little more than two men's frames joined together; it doesn't have the additional bracing tubes you see in the other designs. Two smooth riders on level terrain don't need an internal bracing tube. If I was commissioned to make a light time trial tandem, I would build an open frame. It would be very light weight, and would serve well for the controlled, smooth riding style that time trailing demands.

The designs that follow vary mainly in the way that the internal brace is positioned.

Double Diamond Frame. The double diamond was the first tandem design that really worked. Most of the first "safety" tandems of the late 1880s were double diamonds. All of the English tandems were this design. There are lots of them around, and it is a perfectly functional method of internal brac-

Parts of a Tandem

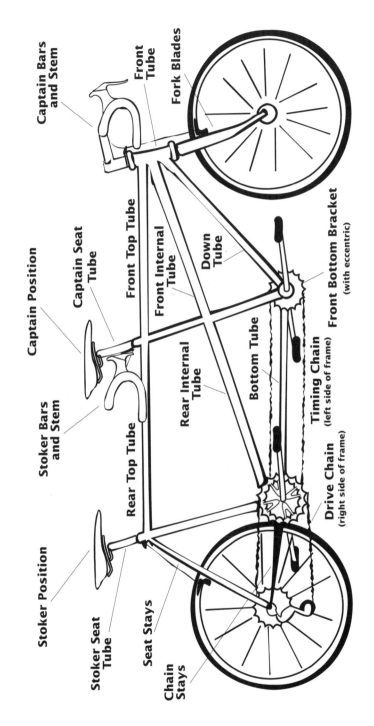

Captain Bars and Stem

Front Tube

Fork Blades

Captain Position

Captain Seat Tube

Front Top Tube

Front Internal Tube

Down Tube

Front Bottom Bracket
(with eccentric)

Stoker Bars and Stem

Rear Internal Tube

Bottom Tube

Timing Chain
(left side of frame)

Rear Top Tube

Drive Chain
(right side of frame)

Stoker Position

Stoker Seat Tube

Seat Stays

Chain Stays

ing. For small tandems, where the captain's seat tube is less than twenty-one inches, a double diamond frame is one of the better designs. The water bottle placement, especially for the stoker, is better than the other geometry's. It also leaves the rear seat tube free for a kidback adapter.

Marathon Frame. The marathon frame probably got its name because the internal brace tube is so long, like a marathon. Certainly not because it is any more suited for long distances than any other design. The marathon frame is widely regarded as the most rigid, even though greater rigidity is produced by greater tube weights and diameters, not only by the design. It is not a good design for using a kidback adapter since the marathon tube bisects the rear seat tube.

Direct Internal Frame. The direct internal tandem frame is a relative new-comer as popular designs go. It was introduced by Santana Tandems in the early '80s. Probably ninety-five percent or more of the tandems being made today are direct internal frames. They easily accommodate kidback adapters, but the water bottle positions are less than ideal for the stoker, who has to reach down almost to the bottom tube to get a bottle.

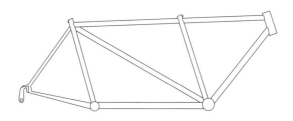

An up tube frame

Up Tube Frame. The up tube design is very new, and was created by Tango Tandems. It is not very common, probably because it is expensive to build and the marginal increase in rigidity is too costly for most riders.

Men's/Mixte Frame. The mixte tandem, though not one of the most popular designs in high- quality tandems, definitely has a place in the market. At Rodriguez Tandems we have made many mixte tandems, and for the riders who want and need them they are absolutely the best design around. The stoker's comfort is the most important consideration in choosing any component, including the frame. In 1990 Schwinn introduced a moderately-priced mixte tandem called the Duo Sport. Burley currently has a frame design they call Mixte X.

Archibald Sharp, in his definitive book on bicycle frame design *Bicycles and Tricycles* (1896), says this about tandem frames:

"Tandem frames may be subjected to considerable twisting strains. If the front and rear riders sit on opposite sides of the central plane of the machine, the middle part will be subjected to torsion. This torsion can be best resisted by one tube of large diameter; no arrangement of bracing in a plane can strengthen a tandem frame against twisting."

One of the common complaints of tandem riders about their tandem is that it is wiggly or that the tandem twists. According to Sharp, all we have to do is put "one tube of large diameter" between those points, and the twisting will decrease. It's easy to see that this is exactly what the marathon design does, and you might call the direct internal a modified marathon. The direct internal is considerably less expensive and easier to build than the marathon, and that probably accounts for its great popularity. It's a good design.

Forks. The fork is just as important as the frame. The fork (and the headset which joins the two) is really part of the frame. Special attention should be given to the fork because its rake (the bend in the blade) finishes off the steering geometry. You have to talk about the head angle and the fork rake together to discuss steering qualities; many enthusiasts compare head angles, but they can't get the whole picture until they take a look at the forks as well.

The curve of the fork's rake and the thickness of the blades combine to give a comfortable ride by absorbing much of the road shock. Next time you go out on your bike, single or tandem, watch the forks flex as you ride.

In the last few years, thanks to mountain bikes, there is a choice of steering tube sizes. I feel that an oversized steerer and headset is appropriate for tandems. Not only is it stronger just at the point where you need the strength, it is more proportional to the size of the bike and the other tubes, so it looks better.

Tandem frames are subject to much more stress than single frames, and should not be made from tubes designed for singles joined into what looks like a tandem. All the major builders have taken lots of time to select their tubes, and when they need to, they make special tubes. Don't buy a tandem made from lugs and tubes and other components that were meant for making single road bikes.

Remove the front fork at least once a year, (or more often if you ride a lot, or you ride off-road) and inspect it thoroughly for any signs of wear or damage. Take a good look at it; catching a crack before it breaks could save you a very nasty accident. At the same time inspect the rest of the frame for hairline cracks, especially at the dropouts and where the chainstays meet the rear bottom bracket.

If your front bottom bracket eccentric is aluminum (most common), do not use Loctite or other glues if you are going to install aluminum cups or rings. Phil Wood makes steel retaining rings for his bottom brackets.

TIG-Welded vs. Brazed Frames vs. Lugs. There are three common ways to join bicycle tubes. Lugging, TIG welding, and fillet brazing are the most common methods of building frames. The last two are used in tandem building, and you'll find enthusiastic proponents of each. Your single bike is probably lugged—the tubes are held in socket joints. Lugs are rarely used on tandems because of a tandem's complicated joints, and because of the huge selection of lugs that a builder would need to have on hand to make all the size combinations. Generally lugs aren't even available for tandems.

One of the two remaining methods is TIG welding. TIG is the acronym for tungsten inert gas. Without getting too complicated, TIG welding combines the technology of both oxy-acetylene welding and arc welding. The result is a high-temperature, tightly-focused flame. The flame melts small portions of both tubes plus a filler rod introduced by the welder. Because the heat is centralized in a smaller area, less time is required to complete a welded joint than a brazed one. The surrounding tubes do not get as hot, and there is less chance of distortion. The benefit is a frame which is lighter, quicker to manufacture, and therefore less expensive.

Fillet brazing, the other method of building tandems, uses oxygen and acetylene to create a lower temperature flame. A filler of melted brass, added in the form of a rod during brazing, joins the two tubes together. Unlike TIG welding, the base metal of the two tubes is not melted. In addition to joining the tubes, the filler flows inside and around the union to create additional support. This excess filler forms the elegant smooth sweep between the tubes which is associated with fillet brazing.

One controversy currently making the rounds of tandeming enthusiasts concerns the benefits and quality of TIG welding as opposed to fillet brazing. Fillet brazing is the traditional method of lugless frame construction. It has been around a long time, it looks very nice, and so far, is generally preferred by tandemists.

TIG welding has long been associated with cheap, foreign-made bicycles. It was a quicker, less expensive way to assemble a bike, but in the past it lacked the quality and endurance of fillet brazing. Recent innovations have greatly improved the quality of TIG-welded joints. Now, while it is still quicker and less expensive, the strength of TIG welding will stand up to any fillet-brazed frame.

There are two chief areas of controversy in TIG welding versus fillet brazing: strength and aesthetics.

Fillet brazing supporters say that the higher temperatures of TIG welding compromise the metal at the union. In fact, the higher heat is applied for only a short time, and does not weaken the molecular structure of the metal. If you have any doubts about its quality, consider that TIG welding is universally used in aircraft construction, an industry notorious for exacting standards.

Aesthetically, many purists prefer fillet brazing because of the classic sweeping curves it leaves at the joint. However, for the curves to look as good as they do, every joint on the tandem has to be ground and filed by hand. This process is time-consuming, and adds considerably to the cost of the tandem.

TIG welding is not as attractive; no argument there. The seams are rougher, but also smaller and less noticeable. A TIG-welded frame is lighter, though, as there is less filler than on a fillet-brazed frame. And all else being equal, the TIG-welded frame costs less.

The aesthetic argument really comes down to personal preference. The reduced cost of a TIG-welded frame is important to some people. But the bottom line is the strength of the joint, and TIG welding and fillet brazing both enjoy a position at the upper end of the welding strength scale.

Seats

The seat is the next most important choice you will make for your tandem, after the frame itself. Seats can be the sole determinant in how you'll enjoy your tandem. No matter how well the tandem shifts, how light it is, or how nice the paint job is, if the seats aren't comfortable, the tandem isn't fun to ride.

Recumbents offer an alternative seating option.

If you have a comfortable seat on your single, put one just like it on your tandem. Our single and tandem seatposts are interchangeable so we can exchange our one-of-a-kind leather seats easily.

No seat should be called a men's or a women's seat. Seats are simply long or short, narrow or wide. Seats have three basic measurements: the length, the width at the back, and the width at the mid-section. Even when two seats have the same basic measurements, the subtle differences in their curves can make one comfortable and the other miserable. Try different seats. You will be able to tell fairly quickly (in a ten-minute test ride) if a seat is going to be comfortable. Don't ever let a salesperson tell you that a foam and nylon saddle is going to break in or feel better later. It's just not true.

Modern seats have four major properties that you should consider (and cost is not one of them): the material of the cover, the material and density of the pad, the material of the base, and the dimensions of the seat. In some saddles the features are combined, as in an all-plastic seat. The plastic is the cover, the pad, and the base. The same is true of leather seats.

The cover is that part which is in contact with your shorts. The cover needs to absorb moisture, and it determines the amount of friction between your shorts and the seat. Not enough friction, and you're sliding all over; too much friction, and the motions of cycling lead to skin abrasion. Common materials are leather and the kind of nylon that Avocet and Spenco use over their gel saddle. There is also vinyl, but only on the cheapest seats. Leather is one of the best covers because it absorbs moisture well and allows a comfortable amount of friction.

Most new quality seats have a padded section between the cover and the base. This padding can be made up of various materials, including soft or hard foam, thick liquid, or gel. The pad should conform to your bottom under the weight of your upper body. It shouldn't be too soft, or your weight will compress it completely and you will be left sitting on the base. It should be firm enough that, by pressing with your thumb, you can't deflect it much.

The base of the saddle is the part that carries your weight and absorbs the road shock. The best bases are nylon, not plastic. You can flex a nylon base, and some are a little thinner in places, so they flex better. The black base on cheap saddles is plastic and it will not bend. Some really cheap seats have a stamped metal base. Ouch!

Considering all features together, the saddle most people prefer has a flexible base, a firm pad, and either a nylon fabric or leather cover. The worst seat would probably be one with a soft pad and a hard base with a slippery top.

Leather seats combine all three functions in the same piece of material. They do break in, which means that after many miles they take on the shape of your bottom. The leather itself is flexible and absorbs road shock. It absorbs moisture, and we think it provides the right amount of friction.

Choosing a saddle is a truly personal endeavor. No two bottoms are the same, and a good seat that works perfectly well for one person can be exquisite torture for another. Try lots of seats, even cheap ones. When you find one you like, stick with it. If your choice is hard to find or out of production, buy a second one when you see it, and keep it put away until you need it.

Angel rides a twenty-two-year-old, all leather Brooks Pro, and he moves it from bike to bike. He also has a reserve one and is beginning to break it in. Carla rides a twenty-five-year-old Brooks Swallow. She has two, one on the tandem and one on her road single, and since they aren't made anymore, she takes very good care of them.

Seatpost

The seatposts have the humble function of holding up your seats. This is a good place to save some bucks. As long as the seatposts are micro-adjustable, they're good enough. The only advantages of the more expensive posts are that they might be a little easier to adjust, and they might weigh a bit less.

The notable exception to the above comment is that the stoker can choose a shock-absorbing seatpost. Carla has one and loves it. It is a Hydrapost and it is adjusted to be rather stiff. The post doesn't move during normal riding, but when we hit a bump the post springs into action. Well, spring is the wrong word; squishes into action is more like it. The post is hydraulically cushioned. As the stoker, Angel always felt comfortable due to the well-designed tandems we rode. But the shock-absorbing seatpost, probably designed with mountain bikes in mind, really smoothes the road. And it helps prevent arguments about "bump" warnings ... hit 'em for all Carla cares!

You can also choose a tandem with an Softride suspension beam. These bikes do not have a rear seatpost. Instead, they have a carbon fiber arm which the seat is mounted on. We have never used one, but in our conversations with other stokers, the Softride beam gets good-to-indifferent reviews. Some stokers like it a lot, and others are more neutral. There is no doubt that the Softride beam is the most effective shock absorber on the market; it just take a bit of getting used to. Some of the neutrality may come from stokers who were not uncomfortable in the first place. Ask yourself if an elegant shock-absorbing system would make your single road bike a lot more comfortable. If you ride long distances the answer might be yes; if you ride only a few hours at a time the answer would probably be no. The reasoning should be the same for the tandem.

Handlebars

Handlebars are pretty high on the list of vital components on any bike, especially a tandem. They might all look the same, but nothing could be further from the truth.

Drop bars have three main dimensions as far as rider fit is concerned: width, reach, and drop. Even when all of the fit dimensions are the same, the bends in the bars are different. The most popular bends are the square ones which have a shorter turn radius, making the bend seem more angular than the bars which curve over a wider radius. The Cinelli #64, from which they modeled their MOD II bends, is an example of this type. These bars offer a long, straight section coming out from the stem with a sharp turn towards the front of the bike and a relatively deep drop before the bend toward the back of the bike. Because of the deep drops, these are better suited for riders with wide palms.

A few years ago Modolo introduced a bar with a straight portion in the drop, and they called the new shape "anatomic." Now SR is making the bend under license. These anatomic bars really do fit better. The SR bend fits smaller hands better than the original Modolo bend.

The captain should choose a bar that is about as wide as his shoulders, and a drop that fits comfortably in his palm. The reach is important, too, but it can be adjusted with the length of the stem to a certain extent.

The stoker will have to make a compromise in the width of the bars. If you choose a bar that matches the stoker's shoulder width, they will be too narrow, and the captain's legs will usually touch the bars where they curve forward. To solve this, several manufacturers, Specialized in particular, offer wider bars in widths of forty-four and forty-six centimeters.

Some stokers like straight mountain bike bars, and some use bars that are bent forward and then up a little bit in the style of track racing "funny bikes." These bars can be made by cutting off regular drop bars and turning them upside down. Comfort is everything, and any-

Straight mountain bike bars are a tandem option.

thing you do to increase comfort is great, no matter what it looks like. In the photos throughout the book, look at the variety of bar shapes and styles that tandemists use. Anything goes!

Tandem Stems

Captain's Stem. The captain's stem is the same as those used on single bikes. You can choose any one at your local bike shop. Strength is important since the forces that are needed to steer the tandem are somewhat greater than for a single. But the difference is not great enough to warrant a special tandem stem, and so they don't exist.

We don't want stems with anything other than a recessed Allen bolt for the stem bolt itself. On some European bikes you might still find the older hex head protruding bolt. If you find a good tandem with the hex bolt, go ahead and buy it, but replace the stem.

Mountain tandems offer stem and other component variations.

You can choose either a road or mountain stem, and they come in all sorts of rises and lengths. The traditional stem is a down-angled racing stem, but more and more stems on road bikes are angled upwards in various degrees, in the style of mountain bike stems. Angel uses an up-angled stem because it feels more comfortable.

If you chose an up-angled stem, and you are going to use drop bars, check to see that the bar-binder portion of the stem is relieved to accept the curves of the drop bars. Since mountain bars are almost straight, the bar-binder section can be narrow, and many will not allow drop bars to be threaded through without modifying the stem.

When you have a custom tandem made you can usually have a custom stem made and painted to match. A custom stem can also be made for any standard tandem, and you can determine the exact stem that you prefer by using a totally adjustable stem. Once you have selected the dimension that you want, have the stem made, painted and installed. Going through this process may seem time consuming, but as in everything else, fit is everything.

Stoker's Stems. We're often asked what the most important aspect of a tandem is, and the answer is always stoker comfort. Stoker stems are part of that comfort. The stoker should not be too stretched out, and conversely, the stoker should not be sitting bolt upright to avoid the captain's back. Unfortunately, there are relatively few choices compared to other tandem parts, and consequently we can discuss nearly every production stem.

Before we get into standard stoker stems we must say that we often recommend having a custom stem made. Most new tandems have a rear top tube that is much longer than those of older tandems. With the right stem, the stoker's reach is comfortable, and not squeezed up against the captain. Some of the older tandems have rear top tubes so short that you can't do anything to make the stoker comfortable. When you are shopping for a tandem, measure the rear top tube from center of seat tube to center of seat tube. If that distance is less than twenty-five inches, take care to be sure there is enough room for the stoker. There is not much you can do with a stem to make the top tube seem longer.

If you are going to have a custom stem made, ask the builder to lend you an adjustable stem. Ride with it for a while in a couple different positions to determine the exact length you want, and then have your stem made.

Unless you ride with many different stokers, there isn't any reason to have an adjustable stem made. Ninety-nine percent of all the adjustable stoker stems we have made for steady teams end up in one spot and never move. If you do need or want an adjustable stem, be sure that the portion that the sliding piece fits onto is not round, even if the surface is roughed up. The bars will certainly rotate unless that piece is angular. Make sure that the rear bars fit the rear stem, and that the seatpost section will fit the seatpost.

Pedals

Pedals are important, not because of their contribution to making the tandem work, but because your feet come in contact with them, and comfort is everything. Having the right set of pedals can help you cover the miles more comfortably.

Pedals can be divided into two categories: those that require toe clips and straps, and those that don't, which are called Clipless. Everyone who rides a quality tandem should use toe clips and straps or Clipless pedals.

The Clipless systems require shoes that have a special cleat that locks into the pedal. When you need to disengage you rotate your foot and it comes out, like boots out of a ski binding. Most of the Clipless pedals are relatively expensive and have high-quality bearings. You can also buy them for their other qualities: their cosmetics, their lightness, or the feeling of being connected solidly to the pedal.

Pedals that are not Clipless can be divided roughly into two subgroups: those that are only meant to be used with racing-type shoes with traditional slotted cleats, and those that are more universal and can be used with non-cleated touring shoes.

The difference is characterized by the width of the pedal and how much it supports non-cleated shoes. In the racing style, the contact between the shoe and cleat is only at the cleat, and the rest of the pedal is cut away to save weight and to get it out of the way of hard cornering.

Other pedals are wider and provide more support for soft-soled shoes, but also have the ridge to engage a traditional cleat if you want to. You need to be concerned with the quality of the bearings and the materials of the axles in these pedals, since many tandem manufacturers choose to save a couple of bucks at the expense of the pedals. Remember, pedals have more to do with comfort than anything else, and if you find that the most inexpensive pedals are the most comfortable, use them.

Captain and stoker pedals don't have to match. Stoker and captain should use whichever pedal is most comfortable for each of them.

Toe Clips and Straps

The primary function of the toe clip is to hold the toe strap up so that you can get your shoe onto the pedal.

Toe clips come in several sizes and shapes. They are made of various materials, and are even available in colors. Nylon toe clips are quite popular. We like the nylon mountain toe-clips which we use on our mountain bikes. Before we went to Clipless pedals, we used the old standby chrome-plated, steel toe clips or the black painted steel clips because they could be bent to fit. You could take that clip that was poking you right between the shoe laces, and bend it to perfection. The plastic ones don't move; they are flexible, but always spring back to the same place.

Some teams like to always have the pedal upright to make it easy to slip their foot in the toe clip. You can attach a small bungee cord from the back of the captain's pedal to the front of the stoker's pedal. Then both sets of pedals are ready to put your feet in. An added benefit is that when the captain is riding without the stoker, the rear toeclips don't scrape on the ground. (This little trick works only when the pedals are in-phase.)

Many riders who don't use cleated shoes use the toeclip to position their foot on the pedal, which is a useful function. However, you should avoid using just any old toe clip, and then shoving your foot in all the way. If you use the clip to help position your foot, make sure that when your foot is in the clip all the way, the ball of your foot is over the axle of the pedal. Try buying a clip that is on the small side, then install the clip with washers between it and the pedal, until it is just the right length. If you have a clip that is a little long, tape any firm padding to the inside where your toe touches, until the ball of your foot is over the axle. With metal toe clips, the rule is to bend them, twist them, and make them fit. The metal is brittle and hard to bend, and sometimes breaks in the process, but with a little care, you can shape them to an ideal fit. When choosing your toe straps, choose a high quality buckle and a strap that doesn't stretch.

Toeclips and straps or Clipless pedals are a must, for safety reasons. They keep your foot on the pedal in the right position, and allow you to concentrate on more important things, like steering the bike or applying power to the pedals without the danger of your foot slipping off. It is not necessary to cinch the straps tight. When we use them we leave the straps loose most of the time, and we can get our feet out easily.

Aside from the safety benefits, toeclips and straps allow you to apply more power to the pedals, and that makes your riding easier and more enjoyable.

Wheels

Wheels are critical to a tandem. An overview of their development, function, and component parts will illustrate why.

The current tandem boom started with improved wheels. From the early 1900s, when the popularity of cycling waned, to the end of World War II, there were really no significant improvements in cycling technology. With the advent of multi-speed hubs and derailleurs, there was a small revival of cycling and tandeming, mainly in England and in Europe.

One of the biggest problems of tandems built after World War II, and before the tandem boom of the 1980s, were the wheels. Most of the wheels just couldn't take the weight of a tandem. A French company named Maxi-Car made a good set of sealed tandem hubs that were strong in every respect. They even made a rear tandem hub with a drum brake that was popular with tandemists between the late '50s and the late '70s. We used them for two years. The biggest problem with these wheels was that they were drilled for twelve-gauge spokes: big thick things with even thicker nipples. So thick, in fact, that they were almost impossible to get through the better rims of the late '70s, which were aluminum with steel ferrules (eyelets) for smaller spokes.

Trying to build a stronger wheel with the same thirty-six spokes as wheels designed for singles by making the spokes thicker was not working. It was difficult to tighten them enough, they flexed, and they broke in an unacceptably short period of time. For a while, we broke spokes on every ride.

In the mid '70s Spence Wolf of the Cupertino Bike Shop in Cupertino, California, began to import alloy rims from Super Champion in France that were drilled with 48 holes. These were coupled to Campagnolo Record 48-hole hubs (which were really factory 24-hole hubs that Wolf had drilled with an extra 24). Using Robergel Trois Etoile stainless spokes, Wolf produced the first strong wheels that really worked on tandems. Soon, Wolf was using sealed bearing hubs made by Phil Wood of San Jose, California. These wheels became the standard of reliable wheels for a long time.

About the same time, Schwinn came out with a great tire, the Schwinn LeTour. With a good sidewall and a raised center, this tire seemed designed for the 16/22 Super Champion rims that were being used on tandems. Tandem wheels were now complete.

Once there were reliable wheels, a few builders, notably Rodriguez and Santana, began to make tandems that were reliable for touring and sport riding. For ten years wheels remained unchanged and manufacturers and builders sold their tandems with 48-spoke wheels. In the last ten years, strong, reliable components have been developed for mountain bikes. Much of the equipment designed for mountain bikes is suitable for tandems, including the wheels and tires, because they are strong enough to withstand the extra stresses of tandeming.

In 1982, Angel designed a tandem around 26-inch rims with 36 spokes. The smaller size tires began to appear in greater variety, and the formula worked well. At the same time, the market shifted from an emphasis on touring to a greater interest in sport riding. People wanted lighter, faster tandems. They began to use 700c rims with 36 holes. It worked, especially on the smooth roads we have in the U.S.

In the ten-plus years since 48-hole wheels came on the market, improvements in materials and rim manufacturing techniques have made them much stronger. Better spokes and stronger hubs and hub axles make 36- and 40-hole wheels acceptable for all but loaded touring or heavy tandem teams. Manufactured tandems are available with 36- or 40-hole wheels, with 48-hole as an option, instead of the other way around. Many of the tandems built at Rodriguez Tandems come standard with 36-hole wheels, narrow 26-inch rims, and tires as narrow as one inch.

Hubs

The hallmarks of good tandem hubs are strength and reliability. Most tandem hubs for 27″ or 700c size wheels have 48 holes, and need every one of those spokes. If you are using 26-inch wheels, strong 36-hole mountain bike-quality hubs and rims are fine. Lately though, because of better rim designs and better materials, some sport or racing tandems are using standard 36-hole single's equipment. We wouldn't use them; the savings in weight cannot make up for the reduction in reliability.

If you are going to buy a new set of wheels for your tandem, the first thing you have to know is the distance between the inside faces of the front and rear dropouts. Most front forks on newer tandems are 100 mm. So most front hubs

Heat sensing stickers

are going have an over-the-locknut measurement of 100 mm. The rear dropouts are a different story, and there is no real standard. Nowadays 140 mm is most common with high-quality tandems, but you should measure yours. Simply remove the wheel and measure the distance between the inside faces of the dropout with a metric ruler.

The reason for such a wide rear hub is that one of the most common third brakes, the Arai drum brake, requires extra space on the left side of the hub. That, coupled with the fact that the rear wheel is stronger when it has less dish (see glossary), makes for a wide hub. One of the drawbacks of such a wide rear hub is that there are not many wide rear axles that accept a quick release, and so most rear tandem hubs are bolt-ons. That is changing, and wide quick-release hubs should be more common soon.

While there are probably forty quality hub makers for single bikes, tandemists have only a few choices. Tandem hub manufacturers include Specialized, Sansin, and Suzue, and the small production makers include Phil Wood, Wilderness Trail Bikes (WTB), and Arvall.

Rims

Selecting tandem rims is not as confusing as choosing rims for a single bike. The tandemist's job is easier, simply because there are fewer choices. Tandem wheels (27 or 700c) usually need 48 spokes, and there is a limited choice of 48-hole rims available.

Before choosing your rims, select your tires. Your rim choice will be easy if you can narrow it down to one or two specific tires you want to use. Use the Tire section to help you select the tire that best fits your riding style. Then all you have to do is choose the material and construction of the rim to suit your aesthetics … and your pocketbook.

In the 27/700c rim and tire combination, there are three tire sizes and two rim sizes suitable for tandeming. For simplicity's sake, we will call the two rim sizes narrow and wide, and the three tire sizes 1⅛ inch (or 28 mm), 1¼ (or 32 mm), and 1⅜ (or 35 mm).

And then there is our favorite: 26-inch diameter rims. Everything is available in that diameter, including the same width choices as in the 27-inch, or wider rims and tires.

Rim Sizes

This discussion on rim sizes applies to all three rim diameters (27-inch, 700c, and 26-inch). Usually you can use two or three tire sizes on one rim size: the one the rim is intended for, and a larger size or two.

Rims have three basic measurements: the width across the outside, the width across the inside, and the depth. Generally, rims are referred to by the inside/outside width. For instance, one manufacturer calls one of its rims a 1622, from the fact that the inside width is 16 mm and the outside width is 22 mm.

Some common sizes for 700c/27 diameter rims:

■ Rims for 1⅛ tires will have an inside width of 15 to 16 mm
■ Rims for 1¼ tires will have an inside width over 16 mm
■ Rims for 1⅜ tires will have and inside width over 19 mm

For 26-inch diameter wheels you have all the above plus rim widths of 20 mm, 22 mm, 28 mm, and more. The tires for 26-inch wheels are not measured in fractions, but rather in decimals, so a 1¼-inch is called a 1.25 inch. (See the Tire section for a fuller discussion of tire markings.)

Once you have made your tire choice, it's time to decide which rim to buy. Now you need to choose material, construction, and finish. Keep in mind that materials are improving all the time, and be sure that your choice is based on current technology. Rims used to be made from softer alloys than they are today, and they were all polished. Now you can get hard alloy rims that are polished, anodized, or heat-treated.

There are four main construction points to be aware of:

1) Cross section. There are several cross sections (see diagram). The box is probably the best of them, even though the double tube is very good and quite common. Other cross sections are aero and concave.

2) Flange shape. We can only recommend a hook-edge type flange. There is also a straight wall and a modified hook-edge. Any high pressure tire requires a hook bead. In the 700c/27 sizes a hooked edge rim tire combination is a must. In the 26-inch arena, there is more latitude when wider rims and lower pressures are used.

3) Joint. There are two types of joints; one is a pin joint and the other is welded. We prefer the pin joint simply because when rims are joined by welding, they have to grind down the weld, and in most cases it can't be smoothed down completely, and the brakes will catch.

4) Spoke holes. The spoke hole can have no steel eyelet, a single steel eyelet, or a double steel eyelet. With thinner light-weight rims we prefer the double eyelet. In many 26-inch rims, which are heavier, the eyelet is not as necessary.

To simplify what we've said above, choose your rim diameter, then choose your tire width, which will give you a rim width. Then choose the material and the construction. Buy the best rim you can afford, with the characteristics you like.

Spokes

Selecting spokes doesn't seem like one of the important choices that you have to make for your tandem until you have to replace a few on the road. Choosing a good spoke is certainly a good investment in the life of a wheel and in the lack of troubles you'll have on the road. For quality spokes, look for both consistency and strength. Strength is important for obvious reasons. Consistency of quality is important because you shouldn't have to wonder when to rebuild a wheel, whether the broken spoke was a fluke or not. Unless you have broken a spoke because of an impact, when the first spoke breaks, the rest are about to break also. We recommend rebuilding the wheel when the second spoke breaks.

Common materials for spokes are stainless steel and plated mild steel. Manufacturers often refer to the tensile strength of their spokes, and it is a good way to compare them. The stronger spokes have the higher tensile strength, which is the force it would take to stretch them to the breaking point.

There is no reason to choose anything but the best spokes. Be sure to have a few extra spokes, and know how to replace a spoke on the drive side of the rear wheel before you take any really long rides. We use and recommend stainless, straight-gauge spokes, either 2 mm or 14 guage, for most tandems. The exception would be for a very light racing tandem where every ounce counts.

Be sure to carry one or two spare spokes. You can tuck them up inside your handlebars and they will be there when you need them. The slight bend will not affect their performance in any way.

You can tell the brand of a spoke by a distinctive stamping on the head of the spoke.

Tires

Tires are a topic of much misinformation and some difference of opinion. With that in mind, we will try to make sense of tire selection. Remember, your choice of tires goes hand in hand with your choice of rims, so read that section too.

The information printed on the sides of tires about size and pressure is totally inconsistent among manufacturers. In some cases, manufacturers aren't even consistent between their own tires. There are some standards and guidelines for manufacturers to fall back on if they choose. The International Standards Organization/European Tire and Rim Technical Organization (ISO/ETRTO) designations have become the *de facto* standard, and if everyone labeled their rims and tires by this method there would not be as much confusion as there is.

If you look carefully, somewhere in raised letters formed right into the tire, you will see a number like 32-630. That is the ETRTO designation. The post-hyphen part of the number (630) refers to the rim size the tire is intended for. In the ETRTO system, all 27-inch rims have a hook edge of 630 mm in diameter (where the tire's hooked bead will seat). They don't measure the diameter of the rim, but rather the diameter of the tire's seating edge. All 700c rims have a diameter of 622 mm, and 26-inch rims are 559 mm.

The pre-hyphen part of the number describes how wide the tire is, and is called the section width. It is the metric measure from bead to bead over the tread, divided by 2.5. It's supposed to be done with the tire maintaining its proper shape over a dowel, but you can come pretty close by flattening a section of the tire and measuring it from bead to bead across the tread. Lay the tire out flat, measure it in millimeters from bead to bead, and divide by 2.5. You should get 32 for a tire that is marked 700c × 32. There is no mystery about it.

ETRTO suggests that your rim can retain a tire that has a section width that is 2.25 times greater than the size of the inner width of the rim. You should pick a tire somewhere between 1.75 to 2.25 times the inner width of your rim. For example, the range of tires that fit on a rim which has an inner width of 16 mm is 28 mm to 35 mm. If you must err, do so on the larger size. Some people go as high as three times the inner width. Choosing a tire less than 1.75 will almost assure you some pinch flats; the tire will simply not give you enough height between the pavement and the rim.

The maximum pressure marking on bike tires is certainly not a performance recommendation, though many cyclists take it as one. If a ninety-pound rider inflates her tires to the 110 pounds maximum pressure, she will have very little rubber contact with the road, the bike will feel unstable through corners, and the hard tires will generally give her a harsh ride. The same tire under a 200-pound rider probably feels mushy and is susceptible to pinch flats.

You should choose the amount of air in your tires based on your experience, comfort, and the road conditions. It does not even have to be the same pressure all day. At the end of a hard day, or on rough asphalt, if you let out a few pounds of air, the ride will be softer. Often cyclists complain that their hands or bottoms hurt. Their first thought is to buy gloves and seats with special pads, and pad their bars. An easier solution would be to let a little air out of their tires, or maybe even use a little wider tire. The loss of speed is negligible.

On a tandem you need good tires with a high profile, since you will need more distance between the road and the rim due to the extra weight of the two riders. There's no magic formula

Counterpoint foot fairing

for the pressure you need. You need to strike a balance between comfort and safeguarding your tires from pinch flats. Inside that range, efficiency is really a minor consideration. Actually, highly over-inflated tires have been shown to be less efficient because they bounce in little skips, losing contact with the road, and therefore losing the means by which the bike moves forward. Captains should listen to their stokers on the subject of pressure in the rear tire; the stoker is intimately familiar with how that tire feels.

Tread patterns have very little to do with performance. Any road tire tread is fine. The only difference you may notice between tire treads is that some are nosier than others. All else being equal, we choose the quieter tire.

Tire life sometimes varies among brands. There is no real formula for choosing a tire that will wear longer, other than proper fit to rim, proper inflation, and avoiding hazards that cut them up!

Twenty-six-inch off-road tires are not particularly good for the road, especially those with high side knobs. You can distinctly feel the movement of the knobs themselves, and it's not conducive to a solid ride. Some off-road tires can even be dangerous while cornering on the road, since they will support the tandem's weight to a certain point, and then side knobs will flex, possibly causing the captain to loose control.

There is very little place in mainline tandeming for one-inch/25 mm and smaller tires. They are just too small to be reliable for the weight of a tandem. If you limit your choice to hooked-edge rims for tandems, as we recommended, that sets a parameter for tire selection.

Tubes

Heavy tubes produce a sluggish ride, not only because they weigh more but because they don't flex.

There are several tube materials. Butyl is the black kind, and the most common. They come in several weights; generally the cheaper ones are heavier. There are good butyl tubes; stick with a well-known name brand.

Latex tubes are light-colored and very light weight. They give a lively ride, but they are somewhat fragile and sometimes fail in ways that can't be fixed; in some cases, though, the tire may have only a small hole, and the latex tube will have a two-inch slit. Latex tubes tend to lose air slowly, so you have to pump up your tires every few days.

Puncture-resistant latex tubes are made in several colors. We like Airseal by Madison. They help prevent flats, and the ride is livelier compared to black butyl tubes.

Another choice you have in tubes is the valve style to use. There are two kinds of valves. The Presta, or French valve, is the smaller of the two, and has a little nut on the top. The Schraeder valve is like the valve on car tires. Riders have all sorts of reasons for choosing one valve or the other. Presta users say their valves are lighter, that they are easier to get air into, and that the larger hole required by the Schraeder valve weakens the rim. The only valid argument is the last, and then only in the narrowest rims.

We use Schraeder valves on all our bikes (we are in the minority these days). During our tandem ride across the country, we discovered that Presta valve tubes were rare unless you were in a big town. But you can buy a Schraeder valve tube at any hardware store. We also like to be able to use the compressor at the gas station.

Recently we have been dusting our tubes with talcum powder. Much of the perceived performance of wheels is in the quality of the tire side wall and the way it moves. Dusting the tube allows the tire and tube to move independently, and you may feel a difference in the ride.

Rim strips

The rim strip goes between the rim and the tube to keep small burrs in the rim from puncturing the tube. There are three common types.

The plastic type rim strip is great. It is usually red, and comes in several widths. It lasts forever and is not affected by heat, age, or multiple installations. Put a pair on your wheels.

The cloth tape or fiber-reinforced tape are second best, mainly because they don't break. Velox is a good and popular brand.

The black, rubber-band type are not recommended for tandem use.

We use Specialized Fat Boy 1.25 × 26 (they should say 32-599) tires, with Madison Airseal Schraeder valve tubes, well powdered. Our rim strips are Specialized red plastic. We generally, but not always, have about 90 lbs. in the front tire and about 100 lbs. in the back.

Headsets

Many riders don't give much thought to the headset. They think that it is the least-moving of all the bearings in the bike, and therefore doesn't do much and isn't very important. However, the headset is the connector between the fork and the frame, and if for no other reason, it has to be of high quality.

The joining of the fork and the frame, the headset connection, is the final link in making a frame feel right. A poorly-designed headset or a poorly-adjusted one makes the frame and the ride feel disjointed, because there will be unwanted movement between the frame and the fork ... not a rattling, loose headset, which is obvious during riding and braking, but rather a headset that has a small amount of motion during cornering or standing up out of the saddle. It has small dents from the balls from day one, and consequently is never quite smooth.

At the same time, headsets should be considered expendable. They wear out. It is the bearings that take the most abuse, since they do not move a lot, and consequently transmit the shock from the road directly and repeatedly. Each ball bearing does not move very much since most riding is in a straight line. The best headset is one with high-quality bearings, and is inexpensive enough to be replaced often. At least replace the bottom cup and cone set.

Any discussion about headsets has to include steerer sizes and stem sizes. Many years ago the French used a 1⅛" steerer that they felt was the proper size for tandems. The walls of the steerer were thick so that it would accept standard size 22.2

mm stem. The headset cup and cone set had a shallow angle, and the whole assembly was machined so poorly that even the best mechanics couldn't adjust them; they always had a loose spot and a tight spot.

Since the oversized system was undesirable, most tandem builders preferred the standard one-inch steerer that was used on singles. The headset was better, but the one-inch steerer required a standard crown, which required the use of standard fork blades, and that made a combination that builders did not really care for. And with good reason; it was too light and the blades moved too much under the stresses imparted by a tandem. Some builders went to the trouble to make their own fork crowns that accepted one-inch steerers and oversized blades, and so made a decent compromise.

That was the standard from 1977 to about 1988, when the mountain bike makers introduced oversized headsets for mountain bikes. They were freed from the limitations of the crown since they preferred the uni-crown construction, where the fork blades are simply bent up to meet the steerer, and welded or brazed on.

The new high-quality oversized headsets that are available now give tandem builders a choice. The proliferation of mountain bikes has interested tubing manufacturers enough to begin mass producing oversized steerers, headsets and fork blades.

Bottom brackets

There are two types of commonly used bottom brackets. One is the sealed type, and the other is the cup and cone type with balls either loose or in retainers. We have used both kinds on our various tandems and don't have a clear preference. If we were to choose one type or the other, we would take a name-brand, high-quality, sealed bottom bracket that is user-serviceable.

Chains

Choosing chains is an easy task. To start with, a well-oiled chain is about 98.5 percent efficient. That's why they have changed so little in the last one hundred years. The weakest bike chain made is strong enough for almost any cycling, so you can hardly go wrong. But you can pay too much. Sedisport is one of the strongest bike chains, is one of the lightest, as well as one of the least expensive. We recommend it in most cases. The exceptions are outlined below.

A tandem has two chains: the timing chain and the drive chain. They perform different functions, and may require different characteristics.

Timing Chain. The timing chain is the one on the left, which connects the captain's cranks to the stoker's. The only reason not to choose Sedisport for your timing chain is if you don't like the way it looks. If that's the case, you should choose one of Sedis' more cosmetically-appealing and slightly more expensive chains. The Sedisport Pro is silver and the Sedisport Gold is gold. All are great chains.

Drive Chain. The drive chain is the one on the right, reaching from the stoker's cranks to the gears. If in doubt about which chain you need for your drive side, buy a Sedisport. It will probably work great. However, if you have a new drive system, use the chain that your system is designed for. In a pinch, Sedisport will work with almost any shifting system.

A chain should last about 3,000 miles. But that depends on how much you ride in your smallest rear cogs, on your riding style (whether you are pushers or spinners), and on whether you're mountain tandeming in the sand and dirt. We change the chain at about 3,000 miles, especially if we are embarking on a long ride and don't want to be bothered by the equipment along the way.

People use the word "stretch" to describe chain wear. However, chains don't really stretch like a rubber band, but rather each pin and bushing wears a little and the collective wear makes the chain appear to have stretched. Park Tool Co. of Minneapolis, Minnesota, has a handy chain wear indicator. By using it, you can change the chain when you measure the wear, rather than just guessing.

Here is a handful of chain tips:

- Any narrow chain will work (more or less) with any shifting system. Any wide chain will work with any wide spacing freewheel.

- Different chains need different chain tools; know yours and carry the right one.

- Oiling your chain every day is not too often. Wipe it down at the same time.

- We replace timing chains about every fourth drive chain.

- Cleaning chains is a waste of time and money. Why spend $20 for a cleaner and $15 for cleaning fluid to clean an old chain? For that much you can buy a new chain. Just oil them regularly, and wipe them down with an old rag.

Cranks

Tandem cranks are essentially the same as single bike cranks. Any crank style could be tapped to fit tandems, but since the demand is so small in the tandem market, compared to the rest of the bike industry, many fine cranks are either not available at all as tandem cranks, or are only manufactured infrequently and in small quantities.

In single bike crank sets the right arm has the "spider" where the chainrings are attached. The crank arm with the spider is threaded with a right-hand thread to accept the right pedal. The left crank is just a plain arm with left-hand pedal threads; that is, they tighten counter-clockwise.

In tandem cranksets, the captain's right crank is a plain crank arm with right-hand threads. The left crank has a spider that will accept one chainring (for the crossover chain), and has left-hand threads. The stoker's left crank is the same as the captain's. The right stoker crank is a normal right crank, with the spider for the chainrings, like on a single bike.

The difference between tandem and single cranks is just in the way three of the arms are threaded. It seems trivial, but in mass production it is a real problem for some manufacturers. To narrow tandemists' choice even more, when manufacturers do make tandem cranks, most of them make 170 mm crank arms, and nothing else.

Cranks differ in the kinds of chainrings they accept. The diameter of the bolt circle (how big the spider is) that holds the chainrings determines the smallest rings that fit. The right stoker crank on all tandems (except on full-time racing bikes) should accept three chainrings. The two-bolt pattern sizes which have the most rings available are 110 mm and 74 mm. Most large crank makers have some cranks in those sizes.

The bolt pattern which is the only sensible choice for most tandemists is the two-bolt pattern of 110 mm for the two outer rings, and 74 mm for the third small inner ring.

Cranks can, and do, break, and you should inspect the crank arms regularly for cracks that may be radiating out from the pedal threads. If the ends of the pedals are scratched, it usually means the tandem has fallen on its side, and is more prone to crank failure. You should take a look at the cranks before any multi-day ride, since a crank failure usually forebodes the end of the ride.

In the early days of the modern tandem revival, many tandems used TA or Stronglight cranks. The most popular was the TA Cyclotourist which came in many lengths and had a lot of chainring choices. They were fine cranks in their time, and though they are still available from some shops and in Europe, modern methods and materials have made new cranks a better choice. If you acquire a tandem with old cranks, we'd suggest that you change the cranks instead of using and maintaining the older set. The older crank sets used crossover rings that were small (30 to 36), which tend to wear out faster, and put higher loads on the bottom brackets.

Chainrings

You should feel free to mix and match rings of any brand in the 110/74 mm bolt pattern. Our own tandem usually has chainrings from three different makers. We also change rings all the time; it only takes a few minutes and makes a big difference.

At the beginning of the season we start with a 52 outer, 44 middle, and 28 inner ring. Later we trade the 52 for a 53, and then finally go to a 54. We also trade the 44 for a 45, and the inner ring goes up to a 30 or 32 by the end of the season. We move back down if we are headed for a mountain tour.

Chainrings are a small investment compared to the tandem itself. Changing your gearing as the season progresses, or if you travel to another area to ride, makes your tandem more versatile.

Chainrings rarely fail, but they do wear out. To help extend the life of your chainrings and freewheel cogs, you should install new chains often.

Brakes

Stopping a tandem is probably even more important than making it go. Downhill, it goes fast all by itself. With twice the mass, only one frontal area, and one set of wheels, a tandem can pick up awesome downhill speeds.

On a tour in the Colorado Rockies, going down Rabbit Ear Pass into Steamboat Springs, we broke our personal speed record at 65.5 miles per hour. Two other tandems also broke 65 miles per hour that day. Rabbit Ear Pass, and most other western highway passes, do not present a challenge to tandem brakes. They usually have gentle grades, open curves, and uninterrupted runouts at the bottom.

Many hills are not so forgiving. They end on an incline at a stop sign which is hidden by the final curve. It is easy to exceed forty miles per hour and have only a few feet of stopping distance.

Most tandems come with cantilever brakes, the same brakes that are used on mountain bikes. Most tandems have the braze-ons for mounting a third brake on the back wheel, usually an Arai hub brake.

We consider the parts of the brakes as separate choices. Choose the brakes themselves apart from the brake pads and the brake levers.

If you are upgrading or choosing brakes for a custom tandem, get the strongest mountain bike cantilever brakes you can afford. Long cantilevers give you maximum advantage. A spiral ramp mechanism generates greater braking power by using the wheel's rotational force to pull the brake pad tighter against the rim while the brake is engaged. The Scott/Pederson brake does the same thing, requiring less hand pressure, and preventing fatigue—a real issue in tandeming. Shimano has some excellent brakes, as do some small production American vendors.

We like pads like Scott/Mathauser or the new Shimano pads that offer a large braking surface. Make sure that the pads do not touch the tire as they wear down. Often brake pads are installed so that when they are new, they work great, but as they wear down, a small lip develops on the pad and that lip eventually touches the tire. A small contact area over a very short period of time is all it takes to blow out a tire.

Brake levers are not only used to activate the brakes, but also provide a resting place for your hands on the bars. They serve dual functions, both of which are important. Most cantilever brakes are made to be pulled by the kind of brake lever you see on mountain bikes, and that style lever pulls more cable than the levers on drop handlebars. Not all drop-bar levers work equally well with cantilever brakes. When you choose a lever, be sure that when the pads meet the rims you still have about three quarters of an inch between the lever and the handlebar. There are special brake levers made for riders with small hands. Angel has small hands and short fingers, and he has to choose levers carefully. There are some levers he can't reach when riding on the drops. Just be sure that if you have small levers, that they do the stopping job.

As we said before, brake levers serve a comfort function, and stokers with drop bars need their brake levers. Dia Compe makes two kinds of surrogate or "dummy" levers. They are absolutely necessary.

For several years we rode with hydraulic brakes. They worked great. Hydraulic brakes eliminate the spongy feeling that is inevitable in a cable that is over six feet long. We used Mathausers, which come factory sealed, so when they're installed on a bike with regular cable guides, it's a somewhat messy-looking arrangement. Magura makes a hydraulic brake that is user-serviceable and the tubing fits in the cable guides on most bikes. We haven't used them, but other tandemists like them a lot.

When stopping 400 pounds of bike and riders, a lot of moving energy is converted into heat, and the rims get very hot. We've seen melted rimstrips and inner tubes, and heard about tires getting soft and coming off the rims. With the proper equipment and proper technique, you have little to fear about stopping your tandem. Make sure that you do not have the black rubber rim strips that come standard on many wheels. Change your tires before you're down to the very last bit of rubber, and if the sidewalls show any cracking from age, change them. Check the treads and side walls for cuts, and check the side walls for frayed or bruised cords.

Don't ride your brakes lightly all the way down hill. Control the speed before going too fast, and if you do have to apply the brakes continually, stop now and then and let the rims and brakes cool off. These are many of the same techniques you use when stopping your car.

We have had heat-sensing stickers on our wheels for many years. A fully loaded tandem making an emergency stop on a very steep hill can raise the rim temperature to 240 degrees Fahrenheit in about twenty seconds. We have never gotten the rims over 200 degrees in the course of normal riding, but other tandemists have raised the temperature of their rims to over 250 degrees on long down hills. Heat-sensing stickers are made by the Markal Company of Chicago.

A third brake, mounted on the rear hub, is a component which is special to tandems. Some tandemists use them, and some don't. You'll hear plenty about both points of view if you spend any time with tandem riders. When Angel was building tandems, every one we made came ready to receive a third brake. This brake is usually a rear hub brake. We tried one for a while and found that we didn't use it. Hub brakes are most useful as drag brakes for long, steep downhills. They generate the same amount of waste heat as rim brakes but the heat is dissipated near the hub where it will not affect the rubber in the tires and tubes.

Many riders control this third brake with a gear shift lever mounted on the front stem. It allows the brake to be set at a steady level while keeping both hands free to use the cantilever brakes as your control brakes. The other approach to controlling the third brake is to have one of the brake levers control both cantilever brakes, and the other lever control the hub brake. However, the double pull brake lever is not really as practical as the shifter approach because on a long downhill, you could have the hub brake on for a long time, and your hand would certainly get tired. More importantly, you give up brake control when only one lever activates both cantilever brakes.

Shifting Systems

One of the best things to happen to tandems has been index shifting. Before, tandems went grinding down the road with the rear derailleur out of adjustment because the captain can't hear the clatter so far back. Adjusting the rear derailleur was a regular topic of conversation. Now a well-adjusted system just slides into gear and stays quiet.

Use the system chain, the system freewheel, and the system derailleurs, cables, and housing. The most important part of index shifting systems are the cable and housing; be sure to use the cables and housings designed for your system.

Many tandemists prefer bar-end or fingertip controls, mounted in the ends of the handlebars. They are good and reliable, but the cable run is long, so they don't shift as crisply as shifters mounted on the down tube. The advantage is that you don't have to let go of the bars in order to shift. We have used both types and feel comfortable with either system. Our tandem now has fingertip controls.

Adventure Cycling Photo by Greg Siple

Kate Brill and Charley Stevenson

Portland, Maine to Seattle, Washington

Kate Brill and Charley Stevenson got up on their unique Counterpoint tandem to ride from Portland, Maine, to Seattle, Washington. As a change of pace, they boarded the 600-foot grain freighter *Kinsman Independent* in Buffalo, New York for an 80-hour passage to Superior, Wisconsin where they resumed bicycling. "Kate and I are both 21 years old and recent graduates of Williams College. Our parents were very apprehensive about this trip. They feared not because of our judgment, but rather because of random acts of violence which occur every day. They feared that we might fall prey to unkind and unthinking people. However, the vast majority of our encounters with people were extremely positive."

Tandem Maintenance and Repair

THIS IS not a maintenance and repair book, so we won't get into the topics that are common to both singles and tandems. Choose any one of several excellent repair books to get a grounding in bicycle maintenance and repair.

A tandem needs all the same maintenance that a single does, with only few additions. The most obvious extra is the crossover chain adjustment. That involves the eccentric, the two-inch aluminum insert in the front bottom bracket shell. The eccentric holds the front bottom bracket and axle, onto which the front cranks are bolted. The eccentric's purpose is to allow the distance between the front and rear crank axles to be varied, thereby adjusting the tension of the crossover chain.

To adjust the tension of the crossover chain, first loosen the eccentric. There are a few different types of eccentrics, and different methods are used to tighten the eccentric in the frame. There are a variety of ways to rotate it. We will assume that you have figured out how to loosen, tighten, and rotate the eccentric on your particular tandem.

Loosen and rotate the eccentric to make the crossover chain tight. Don't tighten the eccentric in this position. Turn the cranks backwards and watch the top of the chain between the crossover rings. Notice that at one point the chain at the top between the chainrings begins to vibrate or tremble. This is the tight spot. This tight spot exists because the chainrings are not round.

You are now ready to adjust the eccentric, since it has to be done at the tight spot. Rotate the eccentric back until you can deflect the chain down about a half-inch where it spans the top of the crossover chainrings. Tighten the eccentric in place.

It is important not to over-tighten the crossover chain. If you adjusted the chain tension without looking for the tight spot first, it would be too tight through the tight spot. The non-stretchable chain will actually bow the frame, and put extremely high loads on the bearings of the front and rear bottom bracket axles and bearings, wearing them out within a very few miles. And, if you placed the tandem under additional

As with all bikes, tandems require regular maintenance and knowledge of component parts.

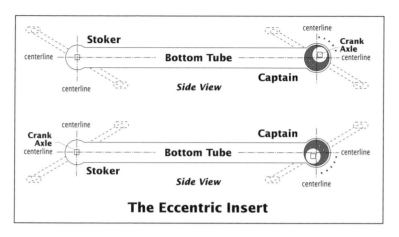

The Eccentric Insert

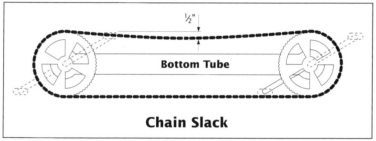

Chain Slack

loads such as standing up on a hill, or sprinting, there is a good chance that the crossover chain would break.

If you complete the adjustment and the difference between the adjusted tight spot and the loose spot is too great (the chain slaps or bounces excessively while you ride), take one of the crossover chainrings off, and rotate it one position ... on the crank spider. If vibration continues then repeat the previous step until you get the least amount of vibration. Replace the chain and do the eccentric adjustment again. This procedure relieves the pressure that occurs when the out-of-roundness of the two chainrings coincide to produce a very tight spot and a very loose spot.

In addition to the eccentric, many tandems have a hub brake which needs special attention. Each brand of hub brake has a different method of adjustment and removal. Become familiar with your particular brake. If you ride in the rain a fair bit, you may have to clean road grit from between the brake pad and the braking surface to quiet the annoying gritty sound. The other occasion you may have to work on the brake is when you have to dismount it to replace a broken spoke. Having to remove the brake while on the road is rare and is a major chore. Usually we would choose to limp home and remove the drum and replace the spoke later.

Most brakes have an adjusting barrel, allowing you to make minor adjustments, and you can tighten or loosen the cable as needed.

As with any bike, take a minute before every ride to do some easy, but possibly life-saving checks.

Check that the wheels are on tight, both front and rear.

Check that the stem and bars are secure. With the front brake on, rock the bike front to back to check that the headset is not loose.

Check that the brakes work and that the pads are not touching the tire anywhere. Spin the wheel to make sure that they are true and that no spokes are broken. Check that you have the proper amount of air in the tires. Take a look at the tread on the tire to make sure that there are no major cuts and that there is enough rubber. Wiggle each wheel from side to side to make sure that there is no looseness in the hub.

Check that the pedals are tight. Wiggle each of the cranks in and out of the plane of the frame to make sure they are not loose.

Wiggle anything that is bolted to the bike to make sure that it is on tightly.

Bounce the bike lightly front and rear by lifting it an inch or two and dropping it to see if you hear any unusual rattles.

The above checks will only take a minute or two and they should become automatic before each ride. You can't afford to suddenly remember to re-attach the front brake straddle cable when you're doing forty miles per hour downhill.

If there is any chance that you will be riding after dark, have lights with you. Riding without lights is probably more dangerous than riding without helmets.

Tom Haltmeier & Denise Daprai, Switzerland

Anchorage, Alaska to Melbourne, Florida

Tom Haltmeier and Denise Daprai are both from Switzerland. They took a long break from their jobs as product manager and secretary respectively for an ambitious tour from Anchorage, Alaska, to Melbourne, Florida. They carried most of their equipment including a spare rim in a Vitelli trailer. Their tandem was a Rodriguez that they bought second-hand in Switzerland.

A History of Tandems

Draisine 1817

Thoughts of tandeming accompanied the first thoughts about bicycling. In 1817, Baron von Drais patented the hobby horse, or Draisine. It wasn't long before cartoons and sketches of two-person machines appeared. The Draisine was propelled by the rider walking or running while straddling the cycle. It had a rudder and a leaning bar for the rider's elbows. Many of the sketches of tandem Draisines are obviously the work of an overly imaginative artist; the contraptions could not possibly have been ridden. Other sketches are of one rider and one passenger. It appears that ladies were not expected to actually propel the cycle.

In spite of many written and sketched references to tandem Draisines, there is no evidence that any were ever built. Baron von Drais continued to refine his invention, and in a 1832 article he mentioned the possibility of adding another seat, "capable of being loaded with other articles, traveling bags, etc." It appears that he had not made a two-seater, and if he did, the seat would not have been for a companion, but rather for cargo. So even though the thought of a tandem Draisine came naturally to builders and observers alike, it is unlikely the thought was ever brought to reality.

Boneshaker 1863

On the whole, bicycle development was at a standstill until about 1863. It was then that the boneshaker arrived. It was the first bicycle that was propelled by pedals. The cranks and pedals were attached to the front hub, like a modern child's tricycle. Otherwise, the configuration was much the same as the Draisine, with the rider perched atop a single wooden or iron beam frame which connected the wheels. Unlike the Draisine, there are existing examples of boneshaker tandems. The wheelbase is the same as for a single, but the frame extends out over the back of the rear wheel, and the stoker's cranks and pedals are attached to the rear hub.

Ordinary 1884

The next development in cycling was the ordinary bicycle, or high wheeler (also called the Penny-Farthing). The ordinary bicycle evolved from the boneshakers as the designers looked for more speed, and to slow the rider's cadence. The cranks and pedals were still attached to the front hub, but the front wheel became huge. The single ordinaries were a bit hazardous, but the tandems were more than doubly dangerous. The main cause of injury on singles was eliminated: being thrown headlong over the front wheel when any obstacle was encountered. The added weight behind the wheel helped keep the rear wheel on the ground. However, many of the ordinary tandems were really little more than connected single bikes, each rider perched over a high wheel, and each steering his end of the tandem. It was the dual steering capability of the tandem that was the downfall of the riders, and eventually of the design.

The first commercially produced tandem, the Rucker Tandem, was unveiled at the annual Stanley Bicycle Club Show in London in 1884. It was like many of the experimental tandems built at the time: two big wheels, each rider propelling and steering his wheel at the hub; the two wheels were connected by a sturdy iron bar. The small rear wheels of the singles had disappeared. One observer, a reporter for the magazine *Cyclist*, saw the Rucker in action, ridden by Mr. Rucker and a skilled companion:

"There is also a horrible engine in existence known as a bicycle tandem. It is formed by joining the large wheels of two full-sized bicycles one behind the other with a stout bar of iron between them, on which two saddles are fixed. It is said to be capable of being driven at a speed exceeding anything else on wheels ... I am bound to add that, with 'the owner (and inventor)

Drawing dates to 1890s

up' in company with some efficient coadjutor, this machine is capable of being handled as almost to convince the spectator that to ride it is neither dangerous nor difficult; but then Mr. Rucker is not only a very clever and very persuasive gentleman, but a first rate rider as well."

The Wright brothers built a similar tandem in 1895, but only Orville, Wilbur, and one other fellow ever mastered "the

monster." A Rucker Tandem replica was built in 1980, but was pronounced "virtually unridable." The major design constraint was the lack of a reliable drive chain. Each rider had to be positioned so that his feet could reach the pedals at the hub of one or other of the wheels. In spite of the difficulties, enthusiasm for bicycling at the end of the 1880s encouraged designers to keep working on the tandem problem.

Moving Towards the Safety 1884

Big changes came in bicycle design, and in tandem design, when the chain drive system was introduced. The riders could be almost anywhere in relation to the wheels, and gears could do the job of the big wheel. An 1888 magazine article displayed eighteen tandem designs, and indeed, the riders were positioned almost everywhere in relation to the wheels. The wheels were a wide variety of sizes, even on the same bike. However, only two of the eighteen put the riders in between the wheels, and then both wheels were driven. Most of the tandems had a wheelbase the same length as a single, with the stoker either ahead of the front wheel or hanging off behind the rear wheel.

None of the designs were very successful. One tandem with a stoker in the back continued to topple backward, though an additional fifty pounds were added to the handlebars up front!

By 1884 distance records were being set on rideable tandems, in spite of the variety of cumbersome designs available at the time. *Outing* magazine reported the first long-distance tandem ride in the United States as 140 miles from Boston to Portsmouth, Massachusetts, and return on May 30-June 1, 1884. Two years later, in June, 1886, Mr. and Mrs. L.H. Johnson rode their tandem 150 miles in twenty hours. They probably took advantage of one of the first modern tandem frame designs. But all bicycles still had hard rubber tires. It must have been a rough 20 hours!

Safety Arrived 1887

In 1887, the first really practical tandems were available: the Psycho from Starley, and the Lightning Tandem Safety from J.W. Hall. Hall stretched the frame of the safety cycle and put both riders between the wheels. Both riders powered the rear wheel via chains and sprockets. Hall even received a patent on his two novel concepts. Steering was linked via rods, and often the frame was designed with the lady's position up front. Often each rider had control of one brake.

Linked steering received poor reviews from avid cyclists who spent many hours on the tandem. They complained that the stoker steered unconsciously, and that by the end of a long day the captain was quite worn out from keeping the tandem under control. By 1897 some tandems had front-only steering, and captain-only braking. However, as late as 1910, one could buy a new tandem with linked steering.

Though tandeming did not grow as fast as cycling as a whole, tandem designs continued to improve, and more companies made them. By 1890, H.H. Griffith wrote in his book, *Cycles and Cycling*, that there were seven tandems which he considered satisfactory machines, though he anticipated a brighter future for tandeming. Robert Scott wrote in 1889 that he found some problems with the "twist of the machine," but nevertheless wrote, "Let the tandem come on; and be received with open arms. Those of us who are a little weak want to make a combination with some flyers, to make up our deficiencies in scorching runs. If we can get on the rear seat and eat dough-nuts part of the time, so much the better."

Pneumatic Tires 1894

In 1894, the pneumatic tire was introduced, and many of the design deficiencies were smoothed out by the more comfortable ride. In 1895 two- and three-speed tandems were available, and the tandem market filled out. Between 1893 and 1900, an American cyclist could choose from among one hundred brands of tandems, with each company offering two or three models. Additional tandems were available in Great Britain. The 1900 Census counted 3,640 tandems built that year. The 1898 figure may have been higher if anyone had counted; the League of American Wheelmen had 100,000 members in 1898, and fewer than half that many in 1900. Bicycle and tandem production may have reflected the drop in the level of interest.

Track Racing and Tandem Pacers

The year 1893 marked the beginning of a new era in professional bicycle track racing, already a popular spectator sport. Tandems began to appear in the pack to keep the pace up and enliven the racing. If one or two tandems in the pack made for more exciting racing, then a pace tandem for each single rider would be even better! Professional teams started employing their own tandemists, instead of relying on the promoter's tandems. Then two-person tandems weren't fast enough, and multicycles of three and four riders were common. Except for steam locomotives, multicycles were the

Tandems are increasingly portable, as is this Montague model.

fastest vehicles on earth. (Some speed records were attempted behind locomotives.)

Next, one tandem per rider wasn't fast enough, and each rider would have two, three, or more pacing tandems and triplets. In 1896 a *New York Times* reporter wrote of a race of four single racers and their pacing machines which included two sextuplets, a quintuplet, eight quads, and "an army of triplets," which amounted to nearly one hundred multicycle riders on the track. Changes of pace cycles during the race were always an exciting maneuver. Moving at thirty miles an hour, and involving the two pace cycles and the racing single, the switch involved up to thirteen riders, and was executed numerous times by each of the various teams on the track, with the other multicycles trying to stay out of the way.

By 1896 multicycle pacing was an important part of track racing; the Dunlop team had 150 pace riders on staff at one point! However, the tracks themselves imposed limits on how long the multicycles could be. The sextuplets were long enough that the front wheel of the tandem was in the turn, and the rear end was still on the straight away. That put extreme stress on the frame, to say nothing of the stress on the captain to force the machine through the curve. The shorter indoor tracks were even more limiting.

When engines developed to the point that they were small enough to mount on bicycles, many pacing machines were motor-assisted tandems. Before long, motorcycles took over the pacing role from multicycles and tandems. For a short time, human-powered tandems made a comeback due to the spectacular crashes that the big motorcycles were sometimes involved in.

Family on tandems

Derailleurs 1933

However, with the decline of cycling in general, just after the turn of the century, tandeming dropped precipitously. In 1933, the *New York Times* announced that a new tandem was in production, and that there had not been a production tandem offered since the 1890s. Any tandeming was done on old bicycles with new components. The resurgence in the popularity of tandeming was due at least partially to improvements in equipment. This time, derailleurs and increased gearing were the breakthrough that gave tandeming a new life, as pneumatic tires had done earlier. A French tandem with a derailleur was available as early as 1925, but tandeming did not enjoy a large number of enthusiasts until the mid-1930s, when cycling events in England were reported to have a high number of tandeming participants.

Modern American Tandems

For many years the large American builders were not interested in building high quality tandems. The "casual tandem," such as the Schwinn Twin, the Varsity, and the Town and Country never disappeared. Tandem riders had their choice of double mixte or men's/mixte. In 1968, Schwinn began to make the Paramount tandem, mainly because they were making track tandems for the 1968 Olympic Team. Predictably, the road tandem design was based on the short, lightweight, and uncomfortable track bike. However, Schwinn dropped the Paramount tandem after tandem events were discontinued following the 1972 Olympics.

The first shop to have any selection of quality tandems in stock was Bud's Bike Shop in Claremont, California. They began importing English tandems in 1972–73. The English had never really stopped making tandems, and in the early 1970s they were making the highest-quality tandem available with existing technology. They were mainly Jack Taylor's and Bob Jackson's. In spite of being the best tandems available, they weren't the epitome of reliability. The components were simply the strongest single-bike parts made at the time. Almost all of the frames were of the double diamond variety. In those years, there were very few American frame builders and even fewer tandem builders.

Before 1976, it was almost impossible to build a reliable tandem, even when choosing parts from anywhere in the world. The only tandem components were TA tandem cranksets, a too-short rear stem made by Pivo, and a great cantilever brake made by Mafac. All the rest of the components were designed for singles, and were just not good enough for the stresses of tandeming. There was also a smattering of "tandem" parts which were not good enough to rely on. As late as 1977, it was not uncommon for us to break a spoke or two on every ride. Tandem riding was a challenge to the road-side mechanic; not many bicyclists thought that tandeming was worth the trouble.

By the mid-1970s tandem frames had been rideable for over 75 years, and now the future of tandeming lie in the availability of reliable parts. The first breakthrough in modern tandem components came in 1976 with the development of a 48-hole wheel by Spence Wolf. He drilled a 24-hole hub with an extra 24 holes, and was able to get Super Champion to drill a few 48 hole rims. Shortly thereafter Phil Wood came out with a 48-hole hub. Combining the new hub with Robergel 3 Etoile stainless spokes produced the first true tandem-strength wheels.

With reliable wheels, real tandem cranks, the Pivo rear stoker stem, and the Mafac H5 tandem cantilever brakes, American frame builders began to make tandems. Santana made their first tandems in 1976–77, and Angel started building Rodriguez tandems in 1977. Other known tandem builders at the time were Jim Bradford and Rodney Moseman. In 1976, 1977, and 1978, there were probably only a hundred or two hundred high-quality tandems sold in the United States. The double diamond was the most popular frame design, with the marathon starting to make inroads.

Mountain bike tandems have grown in popularity since the 1980s.

Mountain Bike Technology

Tandem technology didn't change much until 1983, when mountain bikes appeared on the cycling scene. Manufacturers began to make stronger and more reliable components for mountain bikes. The size of the mountain bike market justified it, where the small tandem market was not able to drive the component industry. Better and nicer brakes began to appear. Good, wide-range triple cranks were designed and made. Strong, rigid, wide-range rear derailleurs were developed. A longer, better-looking rear stem from Santana and Specialized made for even better tandems. In the early '80s Schwinn returned to the tandem market, and in 1988 came out with their current men's/mixte model, the Duo Sport.

Other manufacturers who have contributed to the current popularity of tandems are Kuwahara, Cannondale, and Burley. Quite a few custom builders make tandems. The double diamond and marathon frame designs faded when Santana introduced the direct internal frame. Most builders and manufacturers now use the direct internal design.

Today's tandems are quality machines. You can get one for any special kind of riding you can imagine. They are good-looking, reliable bikes, and the parts are readily available in good bike shops. The current production of tandems for the American market is about 5,000 to 6,000 high-quality tandems per year.

Marianna Di Jorio and Don Sinclair
North York, Ontario

Los Angeles to Colorado to Vancouver to Los Angeles

Marianna, a student of sociology, and Don, on the faculty for computer music at York University, headed east on their Cannondale from Los Angeles to Colorado, back to San Diego, then headed north to Vancouver and back to Los Angeles for a total 6,000 mile trip. En route they were once offered $5 and a "Can this help you any? Buy a few Powerbars maybe?"

Eric and Sally Wang

Los Altos, California

Los Altos, California to Anchorage, Alaska

Our tour started from Los Altos, California and headed north to Anchorage, Alaska. The trip was just amazing! We didn't have enough time to do everything we wanted but it was such a wonderful experience being out there in the vast wilderness ... just us and nature. You can be sure we'll be going back to visit many of these places in the future.

Appendices

Tandem Clubs

Tandem Club of America

The Tandem Club of America (TCA) is an international club for tandem enthusiasts with members in all 50 states and over 15 foreign countries throughout the world. Membership includes a subscription to *Doubletalk*, the bi-monthly magazine.

Tandem Rallies are great fun. We've said it before, and we'll say it again: Tandeming with other tandemists is as good as cycling gets. The rallies listed in the Tandem Club of America newsletter, *Doubletalk*, include the two biggies: the Northwest Tandem Rally and the Midwest Tandem Rally. Others are the New England, the Southwestern, the Southern, the Eastern, Northern Arizonan, and the International Tandem Rally, just to mention a few.

We strongly believe that every new tandem should come with a membership in the Tandem Club of America. There is no better way to find out about the tandem rallies which are held annually all over the country. The bi-monthly publication features articles about touring, traveling, tinkering, and tandeming in all of its aspects.

For information contact: Tandem Club of America, c/o Jack and Susan Goertz, 2220 Vanessa Drive, Birmingham, AL 35242, (205) 991-5519 Fax: (205) 991-7766

The following is a list of member TCA tandem clubs. For current address/phone of each club please contact The Tandem Club of America listed above.

Amicale Des Cyclos Tandemistes
France

Apple Dumpling Gang
St. Charles, MO

Bay Area Roaming Tandems (BART)
San Ramon, CA

Bismarck Tandem Enthusiasts
Bismarck, ND

Carson & Reno Area Tandem
Society (CAROTS)
Carson City, NV

Chicago Area Tandem Society
(CATS)
Barrington, IL

Coalition of Young & Old Tandem
Enthusiasts
Tucson, AZ

Colorado Tandem Club
Fort Collins, CO

Couples on Wheels (COWS)
Brookfield, WI

Couples Riding a Bicycle
Simultaneously (CRABS)
Baltimore, MD

Dallas Area Tandem Enthusiasts
(DATES)
Dallas, TX

Deuces Wild
Las Vegas, NV

Greater Ohioans Advocating
Tandems (GOATS)
Beavercreek, OH

Greater Rochester Eating and
Drinking Society
Rochester, NY

Heart of Dixie Tandems
Trussville, AL

Houston Area Tandem Society
(HATS)
Houston, TX

Lions Tandem Association of
South Africa
Johannesburg, South Africa

Long Island Tandem Enthusiasts
(LITES)
Lake Grove, NY

Michigan United Tandem Society
(MUTS)
Bellevue, MI

New Mexico Chille Peddlers
Albuquerque, NM

Northwest Unofficial Tandem
Society (NUTS)
Seattle, WA

PA. Recreational Riders on
Tandems (PARROTS)
West Mifflin, PA

Paired Iowans Going Somewhere
(PIGS)
West Des Moines, IA

Power (2) Racing Team
O'Fallon, MO

Richmond Area Tandem Society
(RATS)
Richmond, VA

San Diego Tandem Club
San Diego, CA

Tandem Bicyclists of New England
(T-BONES)
Salem, NH

Tandem Club of the UK
United Kingdom

Tandem Club de France
France

Tandems of Indiana (TOIS)
Indianapolis, IN

Team Northwest Tandemonium
Portland, OR

Teamwork Tandem Club
Whittier, CA

Toronto Tandem Co-Op
Toronto, ON Canada

Toucans
Wilmington, DE

Twin Seats
Bellingham, WA

Twin Cities Tandem Club
Woodbury, MN

Upstate (NY) Riders
Ballston Lake, NY

Washington Area Bicyclists in
Tandem (WABITS)
Springfield, VA

Other Tandem Clubs

Austin Tandem Club
1710 Northwood Road
Austin, TX 78703
(512) 478-1337
Contact: Edward Tasch and Anne
Crawford
E-mail: etasch@tenet.edu

Bay Area Roaming Tandems (BART)
PO Box 2176
Los Gatos, CA 95031
(408) 356-7443 or (415) 599-1703
Contact: Bob and Terri Gorman

Couples on Wheels (COWS)
17760 Gebhardt Road
Brookfield, WI 53045
Contact: Bob and Caryl Sewell

Chile Pedalers
PO Box 142
Los Alamos, NM 87544
(505) 662-1429
Contact: Harold and Lynn Trease

Long Island Tandem Enthusiasts
Society (LITES)
56 Pond Path
Lake Grove, NY 11755
(516) 271-0208
Contact: George and Karen Heitman

Modesto Area Tandem
Enthusiasts (MATES)
443 Davidson Road
Modesto, CA 95357
(209) 523-6963
Contact: Lois and Lyndall Frantz

NUTS (Northwest Unofficial
Tandem Society)
5627 University Way NE
Seattle WA 98105
(206) 527-4822
Contact: Estelle Gray

Tandem Club (of the UK)
Penny Farthings,
124 Kings Road West
Swanage, Dorset BH19 1HS
England
Phone: (0929) 422256
Contact: Chris and Jenny Davison

Tandems of Indiana
2164 Golden Oaks North
Indianapolis, IN 46260
(317) 581-1925
Contact: Keith and Janice Conaway

T-Bones (Tandem Bicyclists of
New England)
37 Iron Works Rd.
Concord, NH 03301
(603) 746-4822
Contact: Pat and Dave Berliner

Twin Seats Tandem Club
2900 Lorraine Ellis Ct.
Bellingham, WA 98226
(360) 734-9900
Contact: Kulshan Cycles, or
Jay and Linda Hardcastle

Twin Cities Tandem Club
431 Fontaine Ct.
Woodbury, MN 55125-1440
(612) 735-5102
Contact: Lynn Pagliarini

Other Tandem Contacts

Adventure Cycling Association

The nation's largest non-profit,
membership supported
organization dedicated to
bicycle travel. Produces on-and
off- road touring maps; provides
products, books and maps
through its catalog, *Cyclesource*;
publishes a magazine, *Adventure
Cyclist*; and produces a bicycling
resource directory, *The Cyclist'
Yellow Pages*.

PO Box 8308
Missoula, MT 59807
(406) 721-1776
Fax: (406) 721-8754
E-mail: acabike@aol.com

Association for Blind Athletes
(ABA)
33 N. Institute
Colorado Springs, CO 80903
(719) 630-0422
Provides training, support to
USCF races

Burley Design Cooperative
4020 Stewart Road
Eugene OR 97402
(503) 687-1644

Promoters of The Burley Cycling
Classic (tandems only) and The
Northwest Tandem Rally

Cycle America
Worldwide Bicycling Tour
Directory
(507) 263-2665
Fax: (507) 263-0873
E-mail: cycleam@aol.com
Web Page: http://www.
CycleAmerica.com

League of American Bicyclists
190 W. Ostend St. #120
Baltimore, MD 21230-3755
(410) 539-3399

Tandem Magazine
PO Box 2939
Eugene, OR 97402
(541) 485-5262
Fax: (541) 341-0788
International Quarterly Publication
for Tandem Enthusiasts
Web Page:
http://www.tandemmag.com
Subscriptions: $12.95/yr.
Add $8.00 (Canada)
$20.00 (Overseas)
Contact: Marlen Shepherd

United States Cycling Federation
(USCF)
One Olympic Plaza
Colorado Springs, CO 80909
USCF membership, race
information
(719) 578-4628
Fax: (719) 578-4581
Web Page:
http://www.USAcycling.com

Tandem Retailers

Angle Lake Cyclery
20840 Pacific Hwy. South
Seattle, WA 98198
(206) 878-7457
Fax: (206)-824-3038
Contact: Bob
Complete tandem bikes

Bud's Bike Shop
217 West 1st Street
Claremont, CA 91711
(909) 621-5827
Fax: (909) 625-2063
E-mail: AndyH24@aol.com
Complete line of tandems, parts
& accessories

Collins Cycle Shop
60 E. 11th
Eugene, OR 97401
(503) 342-4878
Fax: (503) 342-4161
E-mail: collins@rio.com
Web Page:
http://www.rio.com/~collins
Complete tandems, parts,
accessories, car racks

Cycle Works
27672 Crown Valley Pkwy
Mission Viejo, CA 92691
(714) 364-5771
Fax: (714) 364-6908
Tandem bike parts & accessories

Cycles, Etc.-Your Tandem
Connection
23882 SE Kent Kangley Rd.
Maple Valley, WA 98038
(206) 432-2820
Fax: (206) 432-6089
TTC custom tandems and
frames, parts and accessories

Europa Cycles & Ski
4302 University Ave.
Cedar Falls, IA 50613
(319) 277-0734
Fax: (319) 277-0739
Contact: Cindy & Russ Dodd
Tandem bikes -Trek, Burley,
Cannondale & Co-Motion

Pedal Power
1944 Rockridge Road
Stone Mountain, GA 30087
(770) 498-2453
Fax: (770) 465-9904
Contact: Karl or Chris
Tandem bikes, frames and
components

Richardson Bike Mart
84 Dal-Rich Village
Richardson, TX 75080
(214) 231-3993
(800) 600-3993
Fax: (214) 234-5724
Complete tandem shop

Tandem Bike Haus
1343 West 18th St.
Merced, CA 95340
(209) 383-4251
Tandem components &
accessories

Tandems East
86 Gwynwood Drive
Pittsgrove, NJ 08318
(609) 451-5104
Fax: (609) 453-8626
E-mail: tandemwiz @ Aol.com
Contact: Mel & Barbara Kornbluh
Tandem parts, crank shorteners,
drum brake removers, car racks,
Pave saddles, free catalog

Tandems, Ltd.
2220 Vanessa Drive
Birmingham, AL 35242
(205) 991-5519
Fax: (205) 991-7766
Contact: Jack or Susan
Large inventory of tandems

Together Tandems
2030 S. College Ave
Fort Collins, CO 80525
(800) 747-2719
(970) 224-0330
Fax: (970) 224-5062
Contact: Chris Lukesic and
Jim Elias
Tandem bikes, components,
accessories and service

Tandem Depot
404 E. Harrison
Royal Oak, MI 48067
(810) 545-5778
Fax: (810) 545-5734
Contact: Jerry Pavlat
Complete line of tandems, parts
and accessories

Tandem Pro
4921 63rd Street
Lubbock, TX 79414
(806) 792-8573
(by appointment only)
Fax: (806) 792-8573
E-mail: cbjuh@ttacs.ttu.edu
Contact: Jurgen
High end quality tandems and
pro parts

Totally Tandems, Inc.
PO Box 702
Ames, IA 50010-0702
(800) 255-0576
E-mail: TTandems@aol.com
Complete tandem supply source,
free catalog

Tandem Cycle Works of Colorado
1084 South Gaylord
Denver, CO 80209
(303) 795-5611
Tandem bikes: Santana, Co-
Motion, Ibis, Bilenky

Wedgewood Cycle
8507 35th NE
Seattle, WA 98115
(206) 523-5572
Fax: (206) 523-6650
Web Page:
http://www.wedgwood.com
Tandem bikes

The Yellow Jersey Bike Shop
660 N. Highpoint Rd.
Madison, WI. 53719
(608) 833-3335
Fax: (608) 833-5438
Web Page:
http://www.execpc.com/yellowje
E-mail: yellowje@execpc.com
Complete line of tandem bikes
and components, service

Tandem Suppliers

3D Racing Frames, Inc.
450 Pioneer Circle
Durango, CO. 81301
(970) 385-7840
Fax: (970) 385-7840
Contact: Chris
Custom tandem frame builder

Advanced Transportation
Products, Inc.
952 Republican St.
Seattle, WA, 98109
(206) 467-0231
Fax: (206) 467-0175
E-mail: ATPVision@AOL.com
"Double Vision" recumbent
tandems

The Tandem Book

Aerolite Manufacturing
1343 W. 18th St.
Merced, CA, 95340
(209) 726-6101
Fax: (209) 726-6102
Twin-Tube Tandems and Aerolite
Pedals

Service Cycle
48 Mall Drive
Commack, NY 11725
(516) 864-2000
(800) 645-5806
Fax: (516) 864-2031
Alleycat pedal trailers

Anew Development, Inc.
1300 NE 48th Ave
Hillsboro, OR 97124
(800) 659-5569
Fax: (503) 693-1057
Draftmaster Sports Racks for
tandems

Angletech
318 N. Highway 67
PO Box 1893
Woodland Park, CO 80866-1893
(719) 687-7475
(800) 793-3038 - Orders
E-mail: anglezoom@aol.com
Contact: Kelvin
Custom tandem and recumbent
bikes and frames

Atoc, Inc.
6615 180th SW
Lynwood, WA 98037
(800) 286-2021
Tandem car racks-"Tandem
Topper"

Bike Nashbar
4111 Simon Rd.
Youngstown, OH 44512-1343
(800) NASHBAR (627-4227)
Fax Orders: (800) 456-1223
Tandem-Tech Assistance: (330)
788-6464
Web Page:
http://www.nashbar.com
E-mail: mail@nashbar.com
Tandem parts, components &
accessories, free catalog

Bilenky Cycle Works
5319 N. 2nd Street
Philadelphia, PA 19120
(800) 213 6388
Fax: (215) 329-5380
Premium hand-crafted framesets

Borthwick Framesets, Inc.
214 Rainbow Drive
Marshalltown, IA 50158
(515) 752-3208
Fax: (515) 752-5541
Contact: Gordon Borthwick
Custom tandem frames

Boulder Bikes
PO Box 1400
Lyons, CO, 80540
(303) 823-5021
Fax: (303) 823-5025
Contact: Rich Williams
Full-suspension mountain and
road tandems

Burley Design Cooperative
4020 Stewart Rd.
Eugene, OR 97402
(541) 687-1644
Fax: (541) 687-0436
Contact: Barry Brown
Tandem bikes, trailers, rainwear,
trailer cycle

Cannondale
9 Brookside Pl.
Georgetown, CT 06829
(203) 544-9800
(800) BIKEUSA
Fax: (203) 852-9081
Web Page:
http://www.cannondale.com
Contact: Customer Service
Tandem bikes, components and
accessories

Chamberlain Cycles
PO Box 55116
North Pole, AK, 99705
(907) 488-7530
Fax: (907) 488-7530
Contact: Frank Chamberlain
Custom tandem builder

Cignal Bicycles
151 Ludlow Ave.
Northvale, NJ 07647-2398
(201) 768-9050
(800) 222-0570
Fax: (800) 238-1959
Entry level recreational tandems

Co-Motion Cycles, Inc.
222 Polk St.
Eugene, OR, 97402
(541) 342-4583
Fax: (541) 342-2210
E-mail: comotion@teleport.com
Web page:
http://www.teleport.com/
~comotion/
Complete tandem
manufacturers, frame builders

CycleTote
517 N. Link Lane
Fort Collins, CO 80524
(970) 482-2401
(800) 747-2407
Fax: (970) 482-2402
E-mail: cycltote@frii.com
Web Page:
http://www.frii.com/~cycltote
Tandem trailer

Davidson Bicycles
2116 Western Ave.
Seattle, WA 98121
(206) 441-9998
(800) 292-5374
Fax: (206) 441-1815
Contact: Bob Freeman
Tandems, racing tandems, etc.

Dawes Cycles Ltd.
Wharf Road Tyseley
Birmingham B11 2EA UK
Products/Services: Bicycle
manufacturer
Tel: 44/21-706-6662
Fax: 44/234-353835
Telex: 337697 G

Fat City Cycles
PO Box 1439
S. Glen Falls, NY 12803
(518) 747-8620
Fax: (518) 747-0250
E-mail fatcity011@aol.com
Web Page:
http://www.cyclelink.com/
serotta/fatcity
Contact: Bela Musits
Serotta titanium tandems,
custom tandems

Green Gear Cycling
4065 W. 11th Ave. Suite 14
Eugene, OR 97402
(541) 687-0487
(800) 777-0258
Fax: (541) 687-0403
E-mail: BikeFriday@aol.com
Tandem Two'sday Complete
Travel System

GT Bicycles, Inc.
3100 W. Segerstrom Ave.
Santa Ana, CA 92704
(714) 513-7100
Fax: (714) 513-7102
7, 21 speed recreational tandems

HH Racing
1901 S. 13th St.
Philadelphia, PA 19148
(215) 334-8500
Fax: (215) 334-3849
Contact: Customer Service
Road and track tandems

Ibis Cycles
PO Box 275
Sebastopol, CA 95473
(707) 829-5615
Fax: (707) 829-5687
E-mail chuckibis@aol.com
Web Page:
http://www.ibiscycles.com
Manufacturer of tandem framesets

Just Two Bikes, Inc.
4821 Washington Ave.
White Bear Lake, MN 55110
(612) 426-1548
(800) 499-1548
Fax: (612) 653-9444
Julie Olson: Manager
Dual recumbent tandems for
recreation, touring

KHS, Inc.
1264 E. Walnut St.
Carson, CA 90746-1320
(310) 632-7173
(800) 347-7854
Fax: (310) 632-3773
Contact: Customer Service
Complete line of tandems

Landshark
225 Crystal Heights Rd.
Medford, OR 97501
(503) 535-4516
Contact: John Slawta
Custom tandem builder

Mandaric Bicycles
1257 Linda Vista Dr.
San Marcos, CA 92069
(619) 736-4427
Fax: (619) 736-4428
Contact: Ves Mandaric
Custom made road and
mountain tandem frames

Meridian Bicycle Works
756 E. Miramar Ave.
Claremont, CA 91711
(909) 626-6832
Fax: (909) 626-6832
World class tandem components

Montague Corp.
PO Box 381118
Cambridge, MA 02238
(617) 491-7200
(800) 736-5348
Fax: (617) 491-7207
E-mail:
Bicycle@montagueco.com
Web Page:
http://www.montagueco.com
High performance, full-size
tandems that fold

Motiv Sports, Inc.
3140 B. Coronado
Anaheim, CA 92806
(714) 238-1000
(800) 229-6684
Fax: (714) 238-1010
Glenn Wilk: Marketing Manager
Mountain tandem frames

Nevil Cycles
112 Timothy Lane
Vilias, NC 28692
(704) 297-5054
Fax: (704) 297-5054
Contact: Customer Service
Full line of custom tandem frames

Otis Guy Cycles
115 Ridge Road
Fairfax, CA 94930
(415) 456-4132
Fax: (415) 453-9650
Contact: Otis Guy
Stock/custom road and
mountain tandems

Outback Bicycles
330 J N. Stonestreet Ave.
Rockville, MD 20850
(301) 309-1950
Fax: (301) 309-1712
Web Page:
http://www.cyclery.com/
outbackbicycles
Contact: David Ross
Custom tandem racing frames

Phil Wood & Co.
580 N. 6th Street
San Jose, CA 95112-3237
(408) 298-1540
Fax: (408) 298-9016
Tandem components

Porter Custom Bicycles
2909 Arno St., NE
Albuquerque, MN 87107
(505) 345-8441
Fax: (505) 345-8441
Contact: David Porter
Tandem road and track racing
frames

Quentin Distributors
845 Carol Ct.
Carol Stream, IL 60188
(708) 653-2929
(800) 323-1741
Fax: (800) 878-3299
Distributors of tandems,
components

R & E Cycles
5627 University Way NE
Seattle, WA 98105
(206) 527-4822
Fax: (206) 527-8931
E-mail: RodTandem@aol.com
Builders of Rodriguez tandems,
components and accessories

Ritchey Design
1320 Hancock St.
Redwood City, CA 94020
(415) 368-4018
Fax: (415) 261-1317
E-mail ritchey95@aol.com
Web Page:
http://www.ritcheylogic.com
Tandem frames and components

Ride2 Tandem Accessories
305 N. 9th Street
Marshalltown, IA 50158
(515) 752-3208
Fax: (515) 752-5541
E-mail: ttandems@netins.net
Web Page:
http://www.netins.net/showcase
/ttandems
Crank arm shortener, tuner
stand, drum brake adjuster

Roland Distributing Corp.
4268 Clark Rd.
Houston, TX 77040-6502
(713) 460-2600
Fax: (713) 690-4252
Contact: R.N. Lo
Complete tandems and rims

Romic Custom Tandem Bicycles
& Frames
4434 Steffani Lane.
Houston, TX 77041-8814
(713) 466-7806
Fax: (713) 466-7806
Contact: Gerry Gasiorowski
Custom tandem bicycles & frames

Rossin SRL
Via Dei Chiosi 11
Cavenago Brianza (MI) 20040
Italy
Tel: 39/2950-1497
Fax: 39/2950-1537
Telex: 326146
Products/Services: Bicycles, frames

Ryan Recumbent Cycles
6 Gigante Dr.
Hampstead, NH 03481
(603) 329-8336
(800) 632-2869
Fax: (603) 329-8336
E-mail:
ryanbike@ryancycles.com
Web Page:
http://www.ryancycles.com
Contact: Karl Ryan
Recumbent tandems

Santana
PO Box 206
La Verne, CA 91750
(909) 596-7570
Fax: (909) 596-5853
E-mail santanainc@aol.com
Tandem bikes, frames,
components and repairs

S&B Recumbent
1607 E. 126th St.
Compton, CA 90222
(310) 762-2243
Fax: (310) 762-2243
Contact: Jack or Smitty
Recumbent tandem builders

Serotta Fat City Bicycles
PO Box 1439
S. Glens Falls, NY 12803
(518)747-8620 FAX (518)747-0250
E-mail serottaone@aol.com
Tandem bikes and frames

SideKids
6717 Palatine Ave North
Seattle, WA 98103
(206) 784-1190
(800) 805-8249
Child's side car for tandems

Specialized Bicycle Components
15130 Concord Circle
Morgan Hill, CA 95037-5493
(408) 779-6229
(800) 245-3462
Fax: (408) 779-7661
Tandem components

Suzue Industrial Co., Ltd.
154, Minami Amabe, Mihara-cho
Minami Kawachi-gun
Osaka 587, Japan
Tel: 81-723-62-1845
Fax: 81-723-62-3245
Tandem components

Tango Tandems
2318 Poppy Lane
Davis, CA 95616
(916) 758-6658
Fax: (916) 758-6658
E-mail:
rpjorgen@wheel.dcn.davis.ca
Contact: Rick Jorgensen
Tandem frame builder

Ti Cycles
824 Post Ave.
Seattle, WA 98104-1419
(206) 624-9697
Fax: (206) 624-9695
E-mail: ticycles@aol.com
Web Page:
http://cyclery.com/ti_cycles
Custom tandem builders-chrome
molly/titanium

Univega/Lawee
3030 Walnut Ave.
Long Beach, CA 90807
(310) 426-0474
(888) UNI-VEGA
Fax: (310) 424-3638
Contact: Customer Service
Makers of several tandem designs

Ventana Mountain Bikes USA
PO Box 39
Rancho Cordova, CA 95741-0544
(916) 631-0544
Fax: (916) 631-7627
Web Page:
http://www.VentanaUSA.com
Mountain tandem frame
builders-full suspension

Wilderness Trail Bikes
187 E. Blithedale
Mill Valley, CA 94941
(415) 389-9050
Fax: (415) 388-7256
Tandem components

Worksman Cycles
94-15 100th St.
Ozone Park, NY 11416
(718) 322-2000
(800) 962-2453
Fax: (718) 529-4803
Rental , 3-wheel, side-by-side
and folding tandems

Zenital, Inc.
10135 Rose Ave.
El Monte, CA 91731
(818) 452-9595
(800) 888-3558
Fax: (818) 452-8333
Complete tandems and
components

Glossary

BOTTOM BRACKET The bearing and axle assembly that holds the cranks on a bicycle.

BOTTOM BRACKET SHELL The part of the frame that accepts the bottom bracket.

BOTTOM TUBE The tube which connects the front and rear bottom brackets. Usually oval. Also called the boob tube or crossover tube.

BRACING Tubes added to the open frame design which strengthen it against twisting motions.

BRAKE HUB A front or rear hub which has a threaded portion on the left side to accept a disc or drum brake. Can also describe a hub which includes a drum brake such as the Maxi-Car or Atom brake.

BUGGER A trailer towed by a tandem or single. Originally "Bugger" was the trailer made by Cannondale.

CANTILEVER BRAKES A type of center-pull brake. They are the brake most commonly used on tandems. They pivot on posts brazed onto the seat stays and fork blades.

CAPTAIN The person who steers the tandem.

CHILDBACK Same as KIDBACK.

CREW The tandem riders; can be more than two if the tandem has more than two seats.

CROSSOVER The drive system in which there are sprockets on both sides of the tandem; one is the drive side, one is the timing side.

CROSSOVER CHAIN The chain on the left side of the tandem which connects the captain's and the stoker's cranks.

CROSSOVER CHAINRINGS The chainrings on the left side of the tandem, connecting the captain's and the stoker's cranks.

CUSTOM TANDEM A tandem made to the specifications of the team who rides it.

DIRECT INTERNAL A bracing scheme that has a tube going from the head tube to the rear bottom bracket shell.

DISC BRAKE A hub brake that has a disc attached to the hub. The brake is activated by another mechanism attached to the frame. Works on the same principle as disc brakes on motor-cycles and cars.

DISH The asymmetry built into rear wheels to accommodate the freewheel and or the hub brake.

DISHLESS WHEEL A symmetrical rear wheel.

DOUBLE DIAMOND A tandem geometry in which the rear down tube is attached approximately at the junction of the front seat tube/top tube at the top, and to the rear bottom bracket.

DOUBLE MARATHON A tandem geometry in which there are two down tubes, one which goes from the head tube to the front bottom bracket, and another which goes from the front seat tube/top tube to the rear bottom bracket.

DRIVE CHAIN The chain that engages the freewheel, and powers the bike.

DRAG BRAKE A brake that is set with a shift lever to maintain a steady friction on long descents. Usually a rear hub brake.

DRUM BRAKE A hub brake in which a drum is attached to the hub, and a pair of brake shoes is attached to the frame. Works the same way as drum brakes in motorcycles and cars.

DRIVE CHAIN The chain on the right side of the tandem, connecting the stoker's cranks to the gears.

ECCENTRIC The aluminum insert in the front bottom bracket shell of a tandem. The eccentric is rotated to adjust the tension of the timing chain.

IN-PHASE An arrangement of the front and rear cranks in which the crank arms on the same side of the tandem are in the same position.

INTERNAL BRACE *See* INTERNAL LATERALS.

INTERNAL LATERALS A tandem bracing system in which two tubes, usually ½″ in diameter, are attached at the head tube, front seat tube, rear seat tube and rear dropout. There can be one tube on each side, twin laterals, or one tube and two extra stays, called third stays. (See LATERALS.)

HUB BRAKE A brake that is mounted to a wheel's hub. Most are attached to the left side of the rear hub, but several manu-facturers make hub brakes that attach to the front hub. Usually controlled as a third brake.

KIDBACK An adapter, usually attached the rear down tube, that puts a set of pedals above the bottom bracket, allowing a child to ride as stoker. The kid-back set usually includes an extra-long stem to bring the handlebars closer.

LADY'S BACK *See* MEN'S/MIXTE.

LATERALS Tubes used to reinforce tandem frames, usually one on each side of the tandem, running from the head tube to the rear dropouts. (See INTERNAL LATERALS.)

MARATHON A tandem geometry in which the bracing goes from the head tube, to the front seat tube, to the rear seat tube, to the dropouts. (See INTERNAL LATERALS.)

MEN'S/MIXTE A tandem geometry in which there is no rear top tube but instead, the back of the tandem is a lady's step-through frame.

MID-STAYS *See* THIRD STAYS.

MULTI-CYCLE A tandem for more than two riders.

ONE SIDE DRIVE *See* SIDE DRIVE.

Open frame A tandem frame design with no internal bracing.

Open rear *See* Open frame.

Out-of-phase An arrangement of the cranks in which the front and rear cranks on the same side do not point in the same direction. (See In-phase.)

Oversized tubes Many tubes on a tandem are larger either in diameter or wall thickness compared to the tubes used for singles.

Partner The other person on the tandem.

Phasing Arrangement of tandem cranks. (See In-phase and Out-of-phase.)

Pilot *See* Captain.

Production tandem A tandem made in a factory, usually comes in standard sizes, with standard components. (See Custom tandem.)

Rear bars The stoker's handlebars.

Rear crossover drive The most common chain arrangement on modern tandems. The drive chain is on the right (from the stoker's cranks to the rear wheel), and the timing chain is on the left (between the captain's and stoker's cranks).

Rear stem The stem that holds the rear bars.

Rear triangle The back of the bike formed by the chainstays, seatstays and seat tube.

Side-by-side A two-person bicycle on which the riders sit abreast. Not technically a tandem. (See Tandem.)

Side drive A transmission system in which all of the chainrings are on the same side of the frame.

Single A bicycle made for one rider.

Single side drive *See* Side drive.

Solo *See* Single.

Stoker The person or persons on a tandem who do not steer. Usually sit in back.

Stoker brake A brake operated by the stoker, usually a third brake.

Synchronizing chain *See* Timing chain.

Tandem A bicycle with more than one rider, one behind the other.

Team *See* Crew.

Third brake An auxiliary brake, usually a hub brake, either on the front or the rear wheel, and operated by either rider as a drag brake.

Third stay Any brace in the rear triangle other that the chainstays or seat stays.

Timing chain The chain which connects the captain's and the stoker's cranks.

Traditional tandem Any tandem made with a frame that is a variation of the open frame design.

Twicer British word for tandem.

Twisting Describes a motion of a tandem frame between the head tube and the rear dropouts.

Up tube An internal bracing tube that goes from the front bottom bracket to the junction of the rear top tube and stoker's seat tube.

Whip Describes one of the motions of a tandem frame, usually the side-to-side movement of the bottom brackets in relation to the top

glossary

Index